GISELE

THE **MARK** OF A LEADER

HAVE FUN CREATING
YOUR GREAT STORY!

THE MARK OF A LEADER

Inspiring Stories of **Ordinary** People
who have done **Extraordinary** Things

Doug Keeley

THIRD EDITION

Canadian Cataloguing in Publication Data
available from Library and Archives Canada

Keeley, Doug, 1953 –
        The Mark of a Leader

ISBN 978-0-978224-1-9-6 (bound)

Published by
The Mark of a Leader, Inc.
Toronto, Canada
www.themarkofaleader.com

Design: Steve Beinicke
Typeset in Adobe Myriad Pro

Printed and bound in Canada
by Docuplex Solutions Inc.

To Pam,
joy in human form

and Matti,
the wise old man cleverly disguised
as a five year old

I love you both

Contents

Introduction

I believe that stories are the glue that binds civilizations and people together. It is from stories that we learn, that we are inspired, and that we grow.

And if there is a purpose to life, surely it is to write the greatest story we can.

Here is a fragment of my story.

On August 12, 2001, my heart stopped beating for just a moment.

Not because of a medical emergency or a world crisis, but because my first child, Matti, just minutes old, opened his eyes and stared at me.

Anyone who has been blessed with children and has been there at their birth will understand this moment.

It is a moment of truth, and in that moment, some would argue, our very purpose on earth is defined. If mine was not defined, it was, most certainly, changed forever.

Before Matti, it had been easy to sit on the sidelines and criticize the game. Now I had a stake in the future – a big stake. Suddenly I was responsible for the development of a child. I knew that for the next 10, 15, 20 years or more this young human would be looking to me, to his mother, and to others for guidance.

But I also knew he would look to the media, to his peers, to the endless sources of input in society today, and be influenced for good or bad.

And as I pondered this, I found myself asking: Who are Matti's role models going to be? Who will be the heroes that he emulates? What stories will shape his character and his path? What stories will bring us together as father and son?

And, for that matter, what stories will shape the lives of those of us who are already adults? We do not stop needing inspiration when we grow up. In fact, I would argue that we need it even more. So where are we to look for inspiration?

Certainly not the mainstream media. I confess that the media had jaundiced me. Want to get depressed fast? Pick up a newspaper.

When I was growing up, politicians, for the most part, were servants of their constituents. Athletes played for the love of the game. Business people were out to make a fair buck, but not at any price.

Read the papers and watch TV these days and you'll see a very different world from the one I just described. Maybe it's because the media appear devoted to bringing us the bad news, not the good. Maybe it's because we have lost our way.

This is not to say that there aren't lots of good people out there, including politicians, athletes, business people, celebrities, cab drivers, janitors, teachers, executives, and so on. They are everywhere, thank goodness.

It's just that crime, cheating, death, disaster, and divorce sell newspapers and magazines and give CNN something to talk about to fill their 24/7 schedule. And so, sadly, those stories shape our world and our view of that world.

It became clear to me that if I was to be the teacher for Matti that all parents should be, it was up to me to provide at least some of the role models.

These role models would be people who do things that make us say, "Wow! How did they do that?" People who make us ask just how good, or how deep, we ourselves are. People who go where others have not gone. People who can ignite our passions.

Good old-fashioned leaders.

So I embarked on this journey. I decided to call it **The Mark of a Leader.** It includes video, audio, multimedia, and event components, and this, the first of our books.

The Mark of a Leader is an exploration. As one of my heroes, Franco Dragone, the brilliant director of Cirque du Soleil, once said, *"People have to be in charge of their own happiness. The only thing we can try to do is reveal to them – offer to them – different interpretations of life – of emotions. Then they are themselves able to find their way to happiness."*

That's what we try to do with the Mark of a Leader program:

present interpretations of life and leadership, in story form, from which you can draw your own conclusions.

I hope they inspire, challenge, and ultimately encourage you to ask questions of yourself, the most important of which is:

"What is the **mark** that I am going to leave with my story?"

What Is This Book?

The Mark of a Leader is a collection of inspiring stories about leaders who have changed the world for all of us.

Some of these leaders are still alive. Some have passed on. Some are individuals. Others are teams. Still others are entire companies or brands.

All of the stories are about ordinary people who have made an extraordinary mark on the world, often against very difficult odds and at significant sacrifice.

The stories are intended to ignite your imagination, make you think, touch your heart, and prompt you to take action.

> • They may prompt you to go to the Internet or a bookstore to find out more about the subjects

> • They may prompt you to change career paths, if you know in your heart that the one you're on is not the path for you

> • They may prompt you to write down a set of goals for

your life and then figure out how to achieve them

• They may prompt you to do that one thing to improve yourself that you have been thinking and talking about, but have never done

• They may even prompt you to go and change the world yourself – to make your own mark

At the beginning of each story, I explain why I believe the story and the leader are important today. At the end of each, I make some personal comments about how the leader has affected me, and I ask some questions the story has prompted me to ask myself - questions that you may want to ask yourself.

What Is the Mark of a Leader?

What is a leader?

If you Google the word, you get a lot of very strange results that are hard to explain.

If you Webster the word, you will find that a leader is "someone who leads." Thanks for that insight.

If you Webster "lead," you will get many responses, but interestingly, they all fall into one of two main categories:

1) to direct the operations, activity or performance of; to have charge of

2) to guide on a way, especially by going in advance. To direct on a course or in a direction

Category 1 is the obvious interpretation of a leader: the most senior person in a hierarchy – a president, prime minister, CEO, general, or the captain of a team. The leader is the person with the most points, money, or votes – the person who comes first.

But I am more interested in Category 2. Those of us with experience in teams knows that the person with the title of leader is not always the person who's really **leading** the team. And it's often the person who says little in the locker room who lifts their team to greater performance by setting a high standard on the field.

How many organizations have you seen where you know that the person with the loftiest title is not really making the tough decisions?

How many times have you heard the phrase, "Behind every successful man/woman is a powerful woman/man"?

I have built and run successful companies and have worked with some of the greatest brands in the world. I am absolutely certain that leadership is the greatest differentiator in business, on teams, and in communities.

But I don't just mean leadership at the **top**. Particularly with the size and complexity of organizations today, success is dependent on having leaders **throughout** your team or organization.

From the bottom right to the top.

In fact, I will argue that when push comes to shove, the organizations with the best and the most leaders working together will win.

How many times have we seen the management of a team fire the coach or CEO and replace him or her with someone new, with no discernible effect on the team's performance? Endless times. Because it takes more than one leader to make a great team.

When I refer to leaders here, of course, it does not simply mean those with title or hierarchy. It refers to people who are prepared to take initiative and to be accountable for everything they do. People who are prepared, in their own style, whatever that may be, to set a standard for others to follow.

Any one of us can lead.

Viewed this way, it is clear that I have seen leaders of all kinds: bold and charismatic; calm and focused; extroverted and verbose; introverted and quiet; sensitive givers and demanding SOBs; egomaniacs and humble servants; entitled, and simply doing their job the best they can.

Some have the gift of the gab. Others lead quietly by example. Some have bold visions of changing the world. Others simply chip away until they make a difference.

Some are natural leaders. Others have to work hard to learn to lead. Still others have the role of leader thrust upon them by life events.

There is no one-size-fits-all answer to the question, "What is a leader?"

Vince Lombardi, the great coach of the Green Bay Packers, said, *"Leaders aren't born, they are made."* I couldn't agree more.

There's no leadership gene. There's no graduate school of leaders.

Some people – kings, queens, and so on – are born into leadership. But these are not the types of people, nor is theirs the type of leadership, that this book is about. Most great leaders in history are ordinary people whose spark has been ignited by something – a vision, a goal, a path – and who have made a conscious choice to follow it in order to do something extraordinary.

Changing the world doesn't happen by accident. Never. It may be sparked by an accident or an incident, but that's all.

- Bob Geldof was watching TV and decided to do something
- Mother Teresa and J.K. Rowling had visions while on trains
- Rosa Parks was on a bus and said, "No"
- Guy Laliberté was traveling through Europe performing on the streets
- Oprah Winfrey was standing on her grandmother's porch and she "just knew"
- Sir Winston Churchill was researching a book and his warrior instincts were aroused
- Candy Lightner lost a child and decided the

tragedy would not be for nothing

Some people had a talent or passion, often from early years, and decided it would be their life.

- Wayne Gretzky had a passion for hockey almost as soon as he could stand
- Tiger Woods was the same with golf
- Richard Branson started businesses as a teenager

There was nothing special in their formula when they were babies. They made choices. They took action, and they were accountable for that action.

And they set out on a journey to make their mark.

Five Common Characteristics of Leaders

If you scratch below the surface of ordinary people who have done extraordinary things, you will find that they have characteristics in common.

At their foundation, as people, they are **accountable** for themselves and their results – there aren't a lot of "victim" leaders. That accountability means they do things – they take **action**. It is part of their makeup.

Without those two ingredients, you cannot be a leader. They are the DNA of leadership.

On top of this foundation, there are five characteristics that are common:

1) Great leaders have a **Vision** of the future – of where they want to be and what they want to do

It doesn't matter whether the vision is to take over the world, to heal the sick in Calcutta, to become history's greatest golfer, to build the neighborhood's best bakery, to win the exotic trip as Best Salesperson, or to lose 10 pounds.

Leaders have to have a clear vision.

2) Leaders **Believe** in themselves and what they are trying to do

Henry Ford is credited with saying some version of this: *"Whether you think you can or think you can't – you're right."* Henry was right.

If Terry Fox had not believed in what he was doing, he would never have taken the first step in his Marathon of Hope. He refused to listen to those who said, "You can't run across a country on one leg."

He believed.

All of us, at some point in our lives, have self-doubt: the voice inside that says, "You can't do that. You're not good enough. You will never succeed." One of the most important skills of leadership is to shut that voice off.

3) Leaders are **Committed**

They persevere. They know that things will go wrong. They

know how to suck it up and keep moving where others are frozen by failure or rejection.

The great Thomas Edison, inventor of the electric light, phonograph, stock ticker, and hundreds more devices, had a wonderful view of why he was so successful. The secret, he said, was that he was better at failing than anyone else. So he could get on with his next attempt faster than anyone else.

4) Leaders have **Passion**

This quality comes from believing in and loving what they do. Passion is contagious. Passion captures hearts and imaginations, and that's what makes people do things.

Bono, of the rock group U2, is one of the world's great passion leaders. Besides driving his remarkable voice and politically charged lyrics, passion moves him to fix the injustice in Africa, to try to bring an end to the famine and the AIDS crisis on that continent. Passion is what gets him meetings with the world's political leaders who can make it happen.

5) Leaders have **Courage**

Leadership is about making tough calls. About getting outside your comfort zone. About doing things that you, and others, have not done before.

About taking risks.

Mahatma Gandhi had tremendous courage, putting his life and those of his followers at risk as he, and they, stood up to British Imperialism and racism in India. He was equally courageous in telling his followers that he, and they, would not fight back, no matter what their enemies did to them. Armed only with courage and their beliefs, they changed the country and the world.

Vision ... Belief ... Commitment ... Passion ... Courage.
Built on a foundation of accountability and action.

Sound simple?

It isn't.

Being human gets in the way, with its fears, its limiting beliefs, and all those people who love to say, "You can't do that. That's Impossible!"

But actually, yes, we can.

Read for yourself ...

The Artists

The Beatles

If there had been no Beatles, no one would have had the imagination to invent such a story.
– Dave Taylor

I have often argued that the greatest service organization in the 20th century was the Grateful Dead. Their customers were so loyal that they named themselves after them – Deadheads. These fans followed the group around the world sleeping in arena parking lots. The band was one of the highest-grossing acts in music, despite having only one Top 10 album in 30 years.

The day your customers name themselves after you or your company, you know you have done your job well.

The Beatles' fans did not name themselves after the group. Instead, the media helped create the frenzy for which they also provided a name – Beatlemania.

It is challenging to find popular music that successfully transcends generations. After all, it is almost a rule that if you like certain music as a parent, your teenage kids won't like it, on principle alone.

The Beatles are an exception. I constantly hear stories of parents whose kids are fascinated with Beatles music and the phenomenon they created.

While the songs may not ignite Beatlemania 40 years later, they do get onto the iPod, and that is no small accomplishment for a band long gone.

That the music and the phenomenon came and went in such a short time is, on reflection, astounding. They came. They conquered. They were gone. Poof! We are all lucky that Mr. Edison invented the phonograph, for the music lives on.

Every company, every brand today, is trying to create the scale of global impact that the Beatles did. Any that succeed will be handsomely rewarded.

What was the secret of their success? How could it be duplicated today? Many have given opinions on this subject, and here is mine.

1961. Rock-'n'-roll was still in its infancy. Music was changing at a blinding speed, causing a generation gap the likes of which had never been seen before.

But most of the action was in America.

In the U.K., the influence of the blues and rock was being felt. But an original, homegrown act had not yet emerged to capture the imagination and trigger the passions of the public.

Then, a tipping point happened.

Two young men met at a church function. One was playing in the band, the other was an attendee who loved the guitar. They started talking, hit it off, and got together after the function to hatch a plan.

They emerged a year later with a group that owed its name equally to Buddy Holly's Crickets and the descriptive term the media were using for the new music being heard everywhere – the "beat" sound.

Perhaps you have heard of their little band – the Beatles.

Let's talk about impact.

John, Paul, George, and Ringo played their first concert together in 1962 in Hamburg. They played their last official one just four years later at Candlestick Park in San Francisco. By then the crowd noise was so deafening there was no point trying to perform in public any more.

They recorded their last album, *Let It Be*, in 1969.

Seven years. Over. Done. Kaput.

In those seven short years, these four working-class young men from Liverpool had changed the world and become arguably the best-known pop band in the history of music.

They made it after being famously rejected by Decca Records as being "just another guitar band whose sound was on the way out." Capitol Records took a chance on them, one of the great decisions in entertainment history.

The Beatles were not just another guitar band. Absorbing everything around them in the musical world – from Chuck Berry to Elvis, the Everly Brothers, and Buddy Holly – they created a sound that was uniquely theirs.

That sound struck right to the hearts of their fans, so powerfully that it induced hysteria.

What was their secret?

Well, clearly, they wrote great pop songs, with catchy riffs and melodies. Lennon and McCartney will go down as one of the greatest songwriting duos in history. And George and Ringo were no slouches either.

At one point the Beatles held all of the top five positions on the Billboard chart and had 12 songs in the Top 100, a feat never approximated before or since.

They had so much great material they helped drive the shift from the single to the LP format. They made an unbelievable 13 albums in just seven years – more if you count all the rarities and oddities. Today, very few musicians make a single album a year, and most of them could not touch a Beatles album for innovation, consistency, and song quality.

The growing popularity of the LP changed radio, giving birth to Album Oriented Radio, or AOR. That one move created the biggest opportunity for new musicians in the history of popular music since the invention of radio itself.

The Beatles broke the mold of pop songs, and not only with the range of styles and sounds they produced. With typical pop songs clocking in at under three minutes in length, "Hey Jude" came in at just under seven. Despite that, it completely dominated the airwaves at the time and gets constant play to this day.

The Beatles also changed album art forever, with breakthrough and divergent covers like *St. Pepper's Lonely Hearts Club Band*, the *White Album*, and *Abbey Road*. Even the simple four-photo layout of the cover of *Let It Be* is still mimicked.

They virtually pioneered rock videos, not as single songs but as full-length feature films like *A Hard Day's Night*, *Help!*, *Yellow Submarine*, and others. In the process they helped pioneer avant-garde filmmaking techniques.

They changed fashion, first with their long hair, tight suits, and boots, and later with their longer hair and outlandish clothes.

When they went to India to study under the Maharishi Maresh Yogi, they brought back Transcendental Meditation, which to this day continues to balance the lives of stressed-out Westerners.

They also brought the music of the sitar and other Indian instruments to the West. One could easily argue that they paved the way for what today is the huge category of World Music.

Their power was so immense that John Lennon once said the Beatles were more popular than Jesus. It was not a popular sentiment in the church, particularly in the southern U.S., where conservative Christian groups organized teenagers to burn their Beatles records in protest.

It may not have been a popular statement, but it was true at the time. With young people, particularly in the U.K., the Beatles **were** more popular than Jesus. But sometimes the truth isn't what people want to hear.

The record burnings were perhaps a sign of worse things ahead for the world's most successful band.

The death of Brian Epstein dealt the group a staggering blow. They lost not only a genius business manager, but also the mediator in the conflicts that always flare up when people's lives are as closely intertwined as they are in a band: Paul and John squabbled about song credits, and George and Ringo wanted more of their songs on the band's albums. And on and on.

And of course there was Yoko Ono. John had every right to fall in love with her. But I think he crossed the line when he insisted that she be given equal say in the making of albums.

George Harrison wrote "All Things Must Pass," and indeed the Beatles did pass.

But 40 years later, a day does not go by that the Beatles are not mentioned somewhere in mainstream media. Their power still holds that strong.

And what can we learn from the world's greatest pop band? What is their mark?

In many ways they were the perfect business.

They had a great product: their songs. It was a unique product – no one wrote and recorded sounds like they did. Those songs touched the hearts of their customers to the point of frenzy.

It was not just that they had a great product. They had a **relevant** product for their market. Particularly in later years, the Beatles became the voice for their generation.

Next, they were geniuses when it came to technology. No one did in a recording studio what they did at the time, and they set a very high bar for everyone who followed. It was just another area where they were ahead of their time, as artists and business people.

They were masters of PR. Their image was carefully controlled and doled out to a waiting market in a highly controlled way. They were also media darlings. Their press conferences were fun, irreverent, and unpredictable. Once again, they created a template for many of today's most popular celebrities.

To their great credit, they were also incredibly likable and down to earth, looking upon their god-like status with a smile and sense of humor. To the public, at least, they were just four nice lads from Liverpool who were fun to be with and who loved life.

They were brilliant marketers. Before them, branded merchandise was a small afterthought to a musician's business, with the possible exception of Elvis. That all changed with the Beatles. Their merchandise came in every conceivable size, shape, and form, and sold like hotcakes to legions of frenzied fans.

But I think the most important mark of the Beatles was how they embraced change. They took chances, tried new things, and listened to everything around them to see what they could learn. They were in a constant state of reinvention and innovation.

If you look at the evolution of the Beatles and their song catalogue, from the first simple three-chord love songs like "She Loves You" through *Sgt. Pepper* to their final works on *Abbey Road* and *Let It Be*, the change is incredible. All through their seven years, they were like chameleons.

Significantly, though, they changed not because the market **forced** them to but because they **wanted** to. Change was in their DNA, and they mastered it.

That's the secret of any great business.

If you want to create a revolution, you have to live that revolution. Whether it's in the world of music or any other business.

Ponderables

There are several lessons from the Beatles that resonate with me.

First, as a business, the Beatles got all the pieces of the puzzle working in sync – the product, the sales and marketing, the timing, and that *je ne sais quoi* called chemistry. It all worked.

Are all the pieces of your business – of your life – working in sync?

With their perfect business they created a revolution – several revolutions, one could argue.

What revolution are you trying to create?

Maybe you don't think of yourself as a revolutionary. The Beatles didn't either. But you wouldn't be reading this book if you weren't interested in improving, in making a bigger impact, in leaving a mark.

I love to look for opportunities for revolution. They are everywhere: in the market, in the way we do business, in the impact we have on our customers' businesses, in our personal lives, in our communities.

Change – be it revolutionary or evolutionary – is part of life. You cannot stop it. So to me, you decide to either accept it – create it – make it work for you, or you will be a victim of it.

I find it useful to ask: What change would I most like to see happen? What could I do to make it happen? And then do it.

Next, the Beatles taught us some great lessons on teamwork.

They showed us how important it is to surround yourself with a great team. The Beatles would not have had the success they did without each other. Chances are we would never have heard of any of them on their own. But together they were magic.

Are you part of a team whose members are indispensable? If not, how could you join or create one?

And, finally, the Beatles showed the fragility of even the best teams. Ultimately they brought their own business to an end, and history will argue that it was well before its time.

Teams to me are like flowers. If you nurture them and care for them, they can become something beautiful.

But neglect them at your peril.

And that's true whether your teammate is in the next cubicle, down the street, or lying in bed next to you.

Chicken Soup for the Soul

*You control your future, your destiny. What you think
about comes about. By recording your dreams and
goals on paper, you set in motion the process of
becoming the person you most want to be.
Put your future in good hands – your own.*
– Mark Victor Hansen

I must confess at the outset that I am somewhat
biased in presenting this story.

First, I am a friend and supporter of Mark Victor
Hansen, co-author of the Chicken Soup series. Mark
is one of the smartest and most enlightened people
I have ever met. He has admittedly made a lot of
money from the series. But he chooses to spend his
time hopping around the world teaching people to
think bigger, to dream, to be positive, and to practice
"enlightened wealth" – making money and giving a
lot back to the world.

This alone qualifies him as a leader. That he, like
most, has struggled through plenty of bad times as
well as good ones makes him a wiser leader.

Second, as you may have noticed, I am a frustrated
consumer of today's media. There is too much bad
news. I am not denying that the bad stuff is happening out there or that we need to know about it. I just
believe it should be balanced by some good news.

I once asked Mark why there wasn't a "good news paper" and he told me that it had been tried, more than once, and had consistently failed. One of his friends had sunk over ten million dollars of his own money into one such attempt. People wouldn't buy the good news.

We're addicted to rubbernecking, and that ain't great folks.

I like good news. I'd be happy if newspapers simply had one section called Good News, filled with stories of successes: saving lives, the millions of people doing good out there, the kids helping old people across the street. I would read that section first and maybe just recycle the rest.

This is a story of two men who went out to create some good news. They almost didn't make it. According to the "experts," the world did not want to hear.

One of the pillars of great leaders, and great brands, is commitment. When things go wrong, great leaders suck it up and keep going. They're clear on their goals, clear on their plan, and refuse to be deterred by setbacks.

For proof of the power of doing this, and also a model for how to start a business from nothing, look at the Chicken Soup for the Soul franchise.

The "Chicken" authors, Mark Victor Hansen and Jack Canfield, are referred to as "the Master of Mindset" and "the Dean of Self-Esteem," respectively. Today they are the most successful publishing team in the world. They are also two of the most influential and successful leaders in the self-help industry.

But it didn't start out that way.

With a BA from Harvard University, a master's from the University of Massachusetts, and an honorary doctorate from the University of Santa Monica, Canfield has academic credentials galore.

Mark has a master's from Southern Illinois University, where he studied under the great Buckminster Fuller. He then went to the school of hard knocks. He began a career as an entrepreneur, went bankrupt, pulled the pieces together, and started his speaking and writing career.

Mark and Jack knew each other from the speaking circuit. Dismayed by the constant barrage of bad news stories in the media, Jack decided to write a book of the best inspirational stories they had heard while speaking around the world.

Jack told Mark his idea. Mark immediately said, *"Great, I'll help you."*

The project began in 1990. Over the next three years they collected and edited their magic number of 101 amazing stories. It had a huge impact on their business – in the wrong direction. It was like a black hole for their energy and incomes.

But they had a clear vision, and they believed in their idea.

Being great believers in visualizing the outcome they wanted, they created a plan. Both had sold many books, but the plan was for this one to be a mega success.

They created a war room, which, according to one estimate, had over a thousand sticky notes on the walls. On the little yellow pieces of paper were ideas for how the book would work:

- Its content – the profile of a story that "fit"
- The audience it would appeal to and why
- How they would get PR for a bunch of "good news" stories
- How to get copies out into stores or other places where people could buy them
- And, most important, their vision of its future

Mark and Jack, never being ones to shy away from lofty goals, started telling anyone who would listen that they were going to sell 100 million books.

Now, let's be clear. Only the Bible sells that many non-fiction books in the Western world. But they believed they could do it – or at least they said they did.

Both deeply spiritual men, they tapped into the power of their subconscious for help. Mark repeated the phrase "mega best-seller" 400 times to himself before going to sleep every night. They both struggled for just the right title to get the books to jump off the shelf, until Jack woke up one night at 4 a.m. to find that "Chicken Soup for the Soul" had come to him in his sleep. There was no doubt that this was the title.

Sadly, most Western businesses today are left-brain dominated. They are driven by logic and spreadsheets, and the power of the subconscious – the unknown – is seldom given a voice. Jack and Mark will both tell you that it was that power that turned their plan into a phenomenon.

So they had a vision. They believed in it. They were passionate about it – and we're talking the passion of two of the world's greatest motivational speakers. But their commitment to the idea had not yet been tested.

Despite already being successful authors, they could not find a publisher who was interested in the project. All the publishers said no one would read good news stories. "That's not what the public wants," they said.

Eternal optimists, the authors did not agree. So they continued their search for a publisher. Meanwhile, they also talked the book up every chance they got. When they spoke, they offered the audience pledge forms to get first copies.

They hired an agent and started doing the rounds of publishers. Here, the myth and reality get blurred. According to Mark, they were rejected by 78 before the agent gave up on them, convinced the product was doomed to failure.

But they persisted.

By Mark's count they were rejected by another 57 publishers before they got a call back from a small company named Health Communications, which was prepared to take a chance on them.

As many as 135 rejections and all those years of work. Would you have kept going?

The deal with Health was not straightforward, though. Jack and Mark had to buy the first 20,000 copies themselves. Talk about a deal with the devil! Fortunately, they had all the names of the people who had expressed interest at their speaking events. They fronted the cash and quickly managed to sell enough books to keep moving.

The first Chicken Soup book was published in June 1993. Word of mouth sold the books at first. Then people started coming back to buy additional copies for friends as Christmas gifts, and the groundswell started. Jack and Mark reprinted. And reprinted.

Then came the "Second Helping," and the phenomenon really took off. Clearly, the books had struck a powerful chord with millions of people.

Perhaps most surprising to everyone was the phenomenal success of the *Chicken Soup for the Teenage Soul* edition. The experts said teenagers would not read good news stories. They were wrong. Stores could hardly keep the book on the shelves, and it remains one of their bestselling titles.

Today, the Chicken Soup series has sold over 110 million books, with over 70 titles in 40 languages. A Chicken Soup title has been on the bestseller lists every year since 1993, and in 1998, seven of them were on the New York Times bestseller list at one time – a Guinness World Record.

Was this success all due to luck? Good timing?
Far from it.

Jack and Mark are two of the hardest-working people in business. By their estimates, they have each given an average of five press interviews a day for the last decade. That's a lot of PR effort. But they knew that, with only a small publisher backing them, success would depend entirely on how hard they were prepared to work themselves.

They passed their original target of 100 million books. Now their target is one billion. No one has ever tried that before.

Looking at their track record to date, do you doubt that they'll succeed?

There are many lessons for entrepreneurs and dreamers in the Chicken Soup story. Stick to your guns. Visualize your success clearly, every day. Verbalize the outcome you want. Create a plan, whether it's with a spreadsheet or a wall of Post-it Notes. Work, work, and work harder. And don't let the begrudgers get you down. It was the combination of all of these that resulted in the Chicken Soup phenomenon.

But what is the mark of the Chicken Soup books? Is it just their incredible sales success?

I don't think so. The series shows us the majesty of the human spirit and the power of that spirit to prevail despite the set-backs life might throw us.

The books have brought fighting families together, healed old emotional wounds, helped people deal with the death of loved ones, created bonds between teens and their parents, and made millions of us laugh, cry, and revel in the simple joy of hearing how other people overcame their obstacles.

In doing so they have helped even the most cynical among us to stop for a moment and do what too many of us have forgotten to do since childhood: simply enjoy a great story.

For that, the Chicken Soup series will go down in history as one of the most important publishing successes ever.

Ponderables

Here are a few thoughts that "Chicken" raises in me.

In the Western world, we are brainwashed into believing that the universe is inherently logical and consciously controllable. But I don't believe this for a moment – nor do many of the world's wisest people.

There is overwhelming evidence that visualizing, speaking, and writing your goals helps bring them to reality. Jack and Mark will tell you it worked for them, as will every world-class performer in virtually any discipline, from sports to the arts. And it isn't hard to do.

First, visualize clearly what you want, and repeat it ritually every day. That sets your subconscious to work.

Then write it, because that makes the connection between your conscious and subconscious.

Then say it aloud, repeatedly, every day. Mark repeated "mega best seller" 400 times every night before going to bed.

There is one other big lesson for me, and that is the practice of being non-judgmental. Every publisher that rejected them **and** their agent were relentless in telling Jack and Mark that the world did not want what they had to offer. How did they know? They just "knew" because they were experts. And they judged "Chicken" as good-hearted fluff that no one would care about.

Their judgment was wrong.

How often do all of us judge other people or their ideas based solely on our personal beliefs or tastes?

Anthony Robbins, arguably the world's greatest

motivator and personal coach, challenges his students to try to go just one day without criticizing or judging anything. Just one day. No judgments. Whatever happens, be positive.

It's hard.

Most people put others and their ideas down because it makes them feel better to do so – it puts them above the others. It's a game of self-confidence and security. But at what price?

Try it. For one day – no judging or criticizing.

If you pull it off, try it again the next.

If you can put many days of non-judgment and "zero criticism" back to back, you're already making a positive difference.

Cirque du Soleil

Logic will get you from A to B.
Imagination will get you everywhere.
– Albert Einstein

In my opinion, great businesses are passionate, emotionally charged, evangelistic, and fun. When you are passionate and you love what you do, it is contagious.

Keeping the passion, the evangelism, and fun gets harder as businesses grow. Bureaucracy, the typical side effect of success, stifles innovation. Frankly, somewhere on the way to the top, most executives lose whatever creativity they may have once had.

Wall Street says they reward innovation, but if the innovation doesn't pay off next quarter, they whack you. Very few brands make the leap from good to great because they lose the spark of innovation along the way.

The exceptions are exciting. They make me stand up and cheer, buy their products and services as often as I can, and pay whatever they ask, if they're in my snack bracket to start with.

Cirque du Soleil is one of the exceptions. It's a story of innovation. A story of young people with a dream who did it not for money, but for love: the love of performing; the love of making people smile and laugh and clap; the love of making them "oohh" and "ahhhh"; the love of seeing people's eyes light up with wonder as their brains ask, "How did they do that?"

The young people who founded Cirque took some great risks, went where no one had gone before, and ultimately turned their love into a magical global empire.

Drum roll, please.

"Ladies and gentlemen, boys and girls, please direct your eyes to the center of the ring. Cirque du Soleil is proud to present The Greatest Show on Earth!"

There are two approaches to creating an enduring and powerful brand in today's competitive market: be the best at what you do, or be the only ones who do what you do.

Cirque du Soleil has done both.

Theirs is a dream that started, like so many, from almost

nothing: a young man in search of his destiny.

Eighteen-year-old Guy Laliberté, an otherwise ordinary middle-class kid from Quebec, Canada, was traveling through Europe armed with little but his accordion, some spoons, and his backpack.

Somewhere along the way, he fell in love – with the art of street performance, and the rich history of the European circus.

When he returned to his native Quebec, he settled in the tiny town of Baie St. Paul, where he found other young people who shared his passions: jugglers, clowns, stiltwalkers, and fire breathers. Among them was a very talented stiltwalker named Gilles St. Croix.

These carefree young performers became a loosely knit troupe, performing on the streets, sleeping in youth hostels or wherever else they could find a room. They lived, literally, hand to mouth while refining their skills.

One day St. Croix set off on a 56 km stiltwalking stunt between Baie St. Paul and Quebec City. As hoped, it got the attention of the media. This brought in a pittance, which the performers used to stage a small street festival.

The festival, while humble in scope, was a crowd pleaser. Its success got the attention of the Quebec government, which gave the troupe $30,000 to create a homegrown circus.

Inspired by the power of the sun, the troupe called itself Cirque du Soleil (Circus of the Sun).

It was a circus unlike any other. It had no animals, no dirt floor, no red-nosed clowns in little cars, no ringmaster in a bad tuxedo. Instead it had acrobats, clowns who were skilled at mime, and hip musicians, all dressed in bright costumes.

This new circus was a big hit in Quebec. But it failed in Toronto and went down the rapids in Niagara Falls. The troupe was technically bankrupt, almost $750,000 in debt.

But guided by a consuming passion and belief in themselves, Cirque did what all leading organizations should do – they reinvented.

They came back a year later with an all-new show called *Magie continue*.

It was a huge hit again in Quebec and, more important, a resounding success in Toronto.

Word began to spread.

Cirque's next show, *Le cirque réinventé*, started to capture attention outside Canada, including that of the Los Angeles Arts Festival. It was time for Cirque to grow its audience.

The Arts Festival did not have the money to bring a circus from Montreal. So Guy Laliberté made the gamble of his life. He called it "to live or die in LA." The deal was that he would pay to get the circus to LA in exchange for top billing and 100% of the gate at their show.

He bet the entire business, because he had enough money

to get his circus to LA but not enough to get it back home. If Cirque was successful, they would make money and be famous outside Canada. If they failed, it was all over: the circus would disband.

Cirque du Soleil was a huge hit, a massive hit. Hollywood stars turned out in droves, word of mouth and television coverage took off, and a new sensation was born.

And thus began what I think of as Cirque's global domination of the human imagination.

They followed this with a string of hits – starting with *Saltimbanco* – that ran through the 1990s. Soon, additional troupes were formed to take Cirque and its seemingly never-ending string of new shows to the rest of the world

Their blue-and-yellow tents were modern versions of the traditional circus tent, minus the dirt floor, the ring, and animals. By eliminating those basic ingredients of a traditional circus, Cirque opened up their shows to new possibilities and new interpretations. Was this really a circus or was it something else?

Before the show, performers worked the crowds, stealing seats, playing games across the audience's heads, and generally creating mayhem to set the mood.

The performances typically started with strangely costumed characters engaged in some kind of struggle with the higher forces of the universe, and their drama would transform itself imperceptibly into a performance of circus feats.

Aerialists would fly through the huge space above the stage. Contortionists would do things most of us thought the human body could not do – yet they somehow conveyed beauty and grace instead of the grotesqueness of the freak show. Jugglers took their art to a whole new level, doing the seemingly impossible. Acrobats turned athletics into art. Clowns performed scenes and dragged bewildered audience members into their mayhem on stage as part of the act.

Performance, tragedy, comedy, and great music all found a home in a Cirque show.

Elaborate sets and complex rigs, a live fusion band, rock show lighting, and special effects lent drama to the show. All were executed to perfection at levels of difficulty that audiences around the world had never witnessed before.

But perhaps the most astounding thing about Cirque was, and is, its universality. *"Our approach was very simple,"* says Laliberté. *"It was about creating a universal language. A show that will be attractive toward every people coming from all over the world. And that was a big thing."*

The performers did come from around the world, and somehow they worked together across languages. On stage they put together a show whose only words were invented gibberish. Yet without the use of language, Cirque told stories that people universally understood. Not only did they understand, but their attention was riveted and they were moved to tears and laughter. Cirque had touched not just their imaginations, but their hearts as well.

Cirque du Soleil had successfully created something entirely new, drawing on many traditions for inspiration but assembling them in a way that was uniquely theirs and remains so to this day.

Cirque quickly became the best in the world – in fact, the only ones in the world doing what they were doing. And that can be a challenge. Competition is what keeps most businesses sharp, and they had no direct competition.

In 1993 entrepreneur Steve Wynn offered them the challenge they needed: a permanent home in Las Vegas for their show *Mystère*. Interestingly, this was after Cirque had developed a concept for Caesar's Palace that their board rejected as "too risky for Las Vegas." Another "Decca decision"!

Freed from the confines of a tent, *Mystère* explored man's place in the universe and pushed Cirque's limits beyond anything they had attempted before. Say what you will about the shallowness of a typical Las Vegas audience, but they couldn't get enough of this new Cirque.

New shows were created. *O*, a show that is largely done in water, and then *Ka*, have set a new standard for live entertainment that will likely be surpassed only by Cirque themselves.

Their most recent venture, developed in partnership with the Beatles' Apple Records and entitled *Love*, is taking Cirque in a new direction once again, with moving projection surfaces and extensive use of video complementing the stage performance.

Today in Las Vegas, the most competitive city in the world for live entertainment, there are five permanent Cirque shows running twice every night except on their "dark" nights. If you want a ticket, order in advance – they're typically sold out.

What other act or company could sell out five different shows twice a night, five nights a week, every week of the year, just a few blocks from each other?

Today, thousands of people per night see Cirque du Soleil in Las Vegas alone. In addition, virtually every night of the year tens of thousands more witness Cirque troupes locally as they tour the world.

Over 30 million people have now seen a Cirque du Soleil show somewhere. Not bad for some crazies from Quebec.

There is no other brand in the world that can claim this kind of live exposure.

Given the awesome power of the Cirque brand and the talent and discipline of their team, it is a safe bet that they will expand into new areas of entertainment soon. Based on their track record, we can only wait with eager anticipation.

And what is the mark of Cirque du Soleil?

I think there are several.

They have successfully created a corporation where innovation thrives. They never stand still, and there are no signs that they will do so in the future. Yet they have done this in an environment that requires incredible discipline and precision.

Marrying innovation and discipline in this way is very rare in business. Yet it is the core of any great enterprise, whether you're in entertainment, pharmaceuticals, or the investment business.

They are unafraid to take risks and have proven this time and time again, starting with their huge gamble at the LA Arts Festival. They are seemingly unafraid to fail. And with every risk they have taken, the door to great opportunity has opened.

They have set incredibly high standards, for themselves and for anyone who ever tries to compete with them. At Cirque, compromise could mean injury or death for a performer, so they simply do not compromise where it matters.

By setting the bar so high, they have attracted the best performers in the world. With the best talent has come the best end product. Every business knows this, but few manage to capitalize on it.

In short, in many ways, they are a model global corporation. They have created an unparalleled sense of team among performers from around the world who must work together while speaking many different languages. They work together in the most stressful environment there is – huge live events – and often with their very lives at risk.

But I think the most important mark is this: Cirque du Soleil has never forgotten what their business is really about. It is not about theatrics or the circus. It is about people.

I believe that inside every human being lives a child. In some of us, the child is forced to grow up too soon. Its imagination is stifled, its sense of wonder beaten away by an often harsh world.

But every time Cirque takes to a stage, that child inside us is allowed to come out and play. And we come face to face again with the simple magic of being human.

> *The next time you go to Las Vegas, or the next time they come to your area, go see Cirque du Soleil. It is the greatest live show on earth. You can find out more at www.cirquedusoleil.com.*

Ponderables

The current statistics floating around the Internet say that, on average, a child laughs 400 times a day and an adult laughs 15 times a day.

I know a lot of adults who don't laugh 15 times a week, so some of us are doing the laughing for a lot of the rest of you!

A Cirque du Soleil show brings out the child in each of us – laughter when the clowns do their thing; "ohhhs" when the acrobats make moves that appear impossible. It is rousing, full-bodied applause all the time, not that polite applause you hear when most politicians speak.

I always carry two lessons from Cirque around with me:

1) Have fun

Having fun is contagious. There is enough sorrow and there are enough grumpy people in the world. We need to balance them out.

There is a payoff, too. People like other people who are fun and funny. You will find that fun will have a positive impact on your business. Even that tough nut from Purchasing or Finance or Legal has a funny bone in there somewhere.

Do something funny today. Or tomorrow. Try it, you'll like it.

2) Take a chance

We all have comfort zones. Where is yours? Take a few minutes to think about what makes you uncomfortable and why, and then deliberately do things to break out of your zone.

I don't mean things like physical danger or horror flicks. Maybe it is speaking in public, or being creative, or a tight deadline, or asking someone out on a date.

Whatever it is, do it. Put yourself at risk.

That simple act will put you in the company of some great leaders.

J.K. Rowling

Destiny is a name often given in retrospect to choices
that were made that had dramatic consequences.
– J.K. Rowling

Imagine a world without imagination.

I grew up in a world dominated by books. I read
every Hardy Boys novel ever written at least once.
Television was in its infancy, so books filled my time.
Books took me into the world of my imagination,
which I filled with images and sounds of my own
creation. Hour after hour. Just like every kid I knew.

Today it is a different world. I am OK with that. But
any of you who are parents or guardians will understand the concern about what many young people
are doing these days. The statistics are scary,
particularly in America.

Try these A.C. Nielsen stats on for size:

- Hours per year the average American youth
  spends in school: 900
- Hours per year the average American youth
  watches television: 1,500
- Average number of hours of television watched
  per person per day in the U.S.: 4

Add to this the time spent playing video games, surfing the Net, and instant messaging, and the numbers are staggering. And then add to that the terrifying fact that the favorite activity for teenage girls in North America is shopping.

Perhaps I am old-fashioned. I accept that. But this worries me.

The negative impact on health by doing little or no physical activity has been well documented. But there is an additional worry to me.

What these activities have in common is that they do little or nothing to contribute to intellectual or creative growth. If this is what our kids are doing, we have every right to be worried.

So when someone comes along and drags kids of all ages away from their favorite thumb-based activity, challenges their reading skills, engages their imaginations, keeps them riveted, and keeps them away from the malls, I stand up and applaud.

When that person is one who went from a broke, lonely, desperate single mom with a dream to an international megastar, despite ridiculous odds, I think that maybe there is a higher power overseeing the forces of capitalism.

And I am encouraged to tell this person's story. Because if you can get tens of millions of kids waiting

breathlessly for a (good) book release, you're making an impact.

Once upon a time there was a girl named Joanne. She was a young, freckly-faced girl of no apparently special attributes. Just an ordinary girl from the south of England.

Shy and not particularly athletic, she loved reading and writing. In fact, she scribbled her first short story about a rabbit with measles by the time she was six. She titled it, simply, "Rabbit."

This ordinary girl lived an ordinary life in England in the 1970s and 1980s, and then went off to college to study French so she could become a bilingual secretary. It was a seemingly perfectly good job for an ordinary girl in Britain at the time.

As much as Joanne loved to study languages, what she really loved to do was write. She started several novels, which she never completed. But she loved telling stories.

Curiously, her life was not really one of great imagination. She had several jobs, as most of us do. The most significant of these was working for a publisher writing rejection letters to aspiring authors who had submitted manuscripts.

As her parents had hoped, Joanne graduated from college and settled down to become a French secretary for the rest of her life, with the hope that a family and children would soon be part of her story.

The flaw in the plan was that being a secretary was apparently not her destiny. She was terrible at it, lacking both the organizational skills and the focus required.

So there she was, armed with a skill she had dutifully learned but with which she was going to have trouble keeping a job.

In her 25th year, an incident took place. An important incident, but one that did not appear to be so at the time. In fact, it was something that happens to every one of us every day.

An idea came to her.

Hers came, curiously, when she was stuck on a train.

Why a train? Why stuck? Why that day? No one knows.

It was the idea for a new story. A story about children who had power and could control their world rather than being controlled by it. The central character in her story was a young orphan who was magically given the chance to go to a special school, where he discovered that he was a powerful sorcerer.

As she had on many occasions before, Joanne started to build the story in her imagination. She gave the character the name of a neighbor she remembered from earlier in her life.

And that was that. Not the first time it had happened. Not the last.

The train system cleared up, the wheels started moving beneath her, and back to reality she went. Joanne's life moved on rather uneventfully. But the story grew in her mind.

She moved to Portugal a few years later to teach English, and there she got married and had a beautiful baby daughter.

She was happy – for a time. But as sometimes happens, the marriage did not survive, and just three years later, Joanne awoke one day to the challenging reality of being a single mother. Surviving as a single mother in Portugal was not an easy path. So she moved back to Scotland with her daughter, into a tiny flat near her sister's house.

It was not a great period in her life. Broke. Depressed by her failed marriage and inability to get ahead. Struggling to put food on the table by teaching French, in Scotland. It was her love for her daughter that kept her going.

So did the story about the young sorcerer. It kept growing, and as it did she wrote it down. Day after day she wrote, often in a coffee shop to keep warm. Not on a laptop and not in a Starbucks. She wrote by hand on pads of paper.

While the world around her was cold and difficult, the world inside her story was one of imagination. While she was powerless in a society that does not do much to help single mothers with limited incomes, inside her story the powers were unlimited. Perhaps the story was an antidote for the real world around her.

The central characters struggled to balance the insecurity of youth with the responsibility of having tremendous power. At every turn there was drama and excitement, conflict and resolution, and fantastic new occurrences. And, of course, there was the ultimate breathtaking triumph of good over evil.

It was a story as old as humanity, but given a new twist, new context, and refreshingly new characters.

And so it went. Year after year for several years.

The Scottish Arts Council was good enough to supplement her desperate income along the way so she could finish her little book. And one day, that's exactly what she did.

She finished and did what all new writers do: she submitted her story to a publisher, hoping it would make that magical transition from a manuscript into a book.

But it was not to be. At least, not immediately. Before her caterpillar could turn into a butterfly, Joanne had to feel the biting sting of rejection, like so many other authors and artists.

"No."
"Sorry, but no."
"It's really good, but unfortunately we cannot proceed at this time."
"It's not the news you wanted to hear, unfortunately. No."
"Thanks, but no thanks."

And on and on.

Until one day, she got this:

"Yes."
Pardon me? Yes?
"Yes."

For her idea on the train and many years of struggle, she received the princely sum of about $4,000. About the same wage as Cinderella got from her sisters.

It didn't matter. Her book had been accepted and would be published by Bloomsbury in the U.K. And in her world, $4,000 would go a long way.

It was 1997. Seven years after the idea had come to her on the train. Seven years of hardship, self-doubt, and wondering where it would all end up. Seven years squeezed out in the form of a story, entitled *Harry Potter and the Philosopher's Stone.*

The book hit the market with a wallop. It was a race to see who loved it more – kids or their parents. Parents suddenly found that their children were more interested in the imaginary world inside this book than the ones in the incessant television shows and video games to which they were all-too-often addicted.

It was a book that kids wanted to read or have read to them! In fact, they wouldn't put it down. How good was that?

In 1997 it was named the British Book Awards' Children's Book of the Year. And not long after, Joanne got a call telling her that the venerable Arthur A. Levine Books, an imprint of Scholastic Press, was picking it up in the United States.

Joanne Kathleen Rowling, the caller said, should quit the job she had teaching French and spend her days doing what she had loved to do since she was five – writing stories. After all, based on how the book was selling, there was sure to be more than just the original $4,000 coming to her.

Joanne went back to her story and churned out the second tale of Harry Potter and his friends. And then another. And another. At a pace of one a year.

Kids, often dressed as characters from the books, lined up with their parents outside bookstores to buy the new stories the instant they came out. Sales shattered every known record for book launches in any category. To date, the books have been translated into 55 languages and sold over 250 million copies.

When movies followed, they simply continued the story of breaking records. The Harry Potter films have brought in billions, and every one sits high on the list of the top grossing movies of all time.

Joanne's story turned from sad to blessed. She became one of the wealthiest women in the world and is believed to be the first author ever to personally earn a billion dollars from writing books.

More important, perhaps, she found love again, remarried, and had a son. And she and her family will live, we hope, happily ever after.

And what is the mark of Joanne Kathleen or J.K. Rowling?

To me, her leadership has been in creating stories that have mesmerized children and adults of virtually all ages, and delivering these stories in book form. Not in short little "read on the plane" books, but in full-length novels that require intelligence, patience, commitment, a vivid imagination, and solid reading skills to navigate.

The power of her stories has dragged kids away from the addiction of violent video games and mindless television, and excited them once again about reading books. She has single-handedly made books "cool" again. (Try to tell me **that's** easy!) She has actually brought some households closer together by reviving the ritual of book reading between kids and their parents or grandparents.

The lesson from J.K. Rowling is more subtle, however.

It is estimated that each of us has 60,000 thoughts every day. Most of them come and go, often ignored. We let them pass, because we are too busy, because we do not think we could do anything with them. For whatever reason, we let them go.

J.K. Rowling took just one of her ideas and did not let it go. Despite her circumstances, she turned that little idea into the most remarkable publishing phenomenon of the 20th century.

And in so doing, got tens of millions of kids excited again about reading books.

On behalf of parents around the world, I say, "Thank you, J.K."

And we hope, for her, that it is undoubtedly not ... **The End**

Ponderables

Like Chicken Soup for the Soul, the story of Harry Potter is one of believing in yourself. But the lesson is very different for me.

We all have ideas, all day. For some, the ideas are like a river – they never stop coming. For others, ideas are hard work. But we all have them.

How many times have you seen a product and had déjà vu because you had the idea once yourself? You kick yourself and say, "Why didn't I do that?"

It might be a book. It might be a kitchen device in a store. It might be a movie. It doesn't matter. It is an idea that someone else took from the idea stage and brought to life. And you didn't.

Most everyone I know can relate to this.

How many ideas have you had that inspired you – that made you think, "That's a great idea!" – but didn't act upon? How many of those ideas are still waiting to be brought to life?

Do you remember them? Could you bring them to life now?

Sir Richard Branson says he carries a notepad with him to capture his ideas. Many others carry a small voice recorder. I send myself a lot of reminders on my Blackberry.

It doesn't matter how you do it. Just do it.

The only difference between the inventors, the artists, the authors, the creators, and most of us is that they didn't stop at just having an idea. They had the moxie, passion, and commitment to bring those ideas to life.

And every one of you can, too.

Miles Davis

Do not fear mistakes.
There are none.
– Miles Davis

Some people suggest that the symphony orchestra is a good metaphor for teamwork in the corporate world. Wrong, wrong, wrong!

In a symphony orchestra there is one leader and a stage full of followers who read the notes and interpret them with only minor variation. That is the exact opposite of what leadership cultures should be. If a leader has to tell everyone exactly what to do, the organization is doomed to failure.

The music metaphor that **does** work for corporate teams is jazz.

In small group jazz, a song is just a sketch. It is a set of chord changes with a melody. The group, with direction from the leader, decides the groove or feel and the style or "color" they want to play it – fast or slow, aggressive or relaxed, Latin, swing, rock, or reggae, "straight" or "out there." The style or color determines how each member will play.

In corporate terms, they agree on the vision, they agree on the structure, and then they have almost infinite freedom to listen, support each other, and take the music where they collectively feel it should go.

Some groups turn this into sophisticated organized chaos. Others are more traditional. But the music and the interpretation – the length of the song and where it will go – is entirely up to the performers.

You cannot be a good jazz player without being a good listener. And you cannot be a good leader without being a good listener as well.

You think your business is competitive. Try being a musician.

You might laugh and think, "Sex, drugs, rock-'n'-roll, sleeping till noon – how bad is that?"

But think about it. How many guitar players are there in the world – half a billion? Ditto for aspiring singers. How many new bands start in a garage or a basement every year hoping to be the next U2 or Green Day? A few million?

And how many of them make it? A few. How many songs or CDs did you buy last year from new artists?

Probably not many.

But even more interesting to me is the fact that in the Western musical system there are only 12 notes. That's it.

When was the last time you heard an interview with Bono where he said, "The last album wasn't very strong because we've used all those notes before. We need some new notes"?

Musicians make do with what they have. And here is what they have:

1) Their choice of instruments
2) Their choice of notes
3) How they string those notes together – melody and harmony – from the same 12 notes
4) The rhythm they put to them

And then the subtle differentiators between the good and the great:

5) The shape of the notes
6) The space between the notes

The shape of a note is what gives it its character. Attack it, bend it, vibrato it, slur it, slide in, slide out, roll it, mute it. These give a note its defining sound.

You can identify a great musician with one or two notes because each musician has a sound that is completely personal. Carlos Santana is a great example: one note and it is unmistakably him.

The space between notes is more complex though. Most musicians are about as comfortable with it as most people are with pauses in conversations: not very.

In a typical conversation, if there is a lull, someone jumps in to fill the air. If there's a lot of quiet, most people are uncomfortable.

What made Miles Davis so remarkable is that he was comfortable with the spaces. This is what he said about musicianship: *"Don't play what's there. Play what isn't there."*

Miles is generally regarded as one of the most important musicians of the 20th century and in all of jazz history. He was a rarity: a black kid from a wealthy family who was encouraged – no, allowed – to take music seriously. His dental surgeon father gave him a trumpet at age 13, and that was that. Goodbye, world. Two years later he was playing with local bands.

Miles was one of the lucky ones. He was enrolled at the Juilliard School of Music in New York, arguably the best music school in the world.

While he was studying there, most jazzers were struggling to get by. Drugs were everywhere on the jazz scene, and any income from gigs or records all too often disappeared into a drink glass, up a nose, or into a vein.

At the time, in the mid-1940s, bebop was the emerging jazz style. Charlie "Bird" Parker and Dizzy Gillespie were the gods of bop, a terrifying new style that pushed the limits of harmony and technique beyond what anyone had ever imagined before.

Bird and Diz were master players. With their peers they would play blisteringly fast tempos and complex chord changes that would quickly sort out the real players from the wannabes.

Here is how it worked. Aspiring young musicians would come to the clubs at night with their instruments. If they were lucky, they might be allowed to sit in on a tune. It was how new talent broke into the scene.

It was into this world that Miles Davis entered when he dropped out of Juilliard, to his parents' chagrin, and took to the streets of New York before he had even turned 20.

Miles couldn't keep up with Bird or Diz. They were too good, too fast. The difference between him and every other kid was that he knew it. He was on stage with Diz, one of the greatest trumpet players ever. What was he going to do – try to outplay him?

While his mentors were playing lines of notes that rode like roller coasters on top of the rhythm section, Miles began to go a different route. He focused on the shape of his notes, and the spaces between them.

Over the next few years, with a variety of bands, he found that he could create a whole new feel for a song simply by opening up. It was like doing yoga in a room full of sweaty weightlifters.

He would let long stretches of time go by with silence, then sneak his way back in with a note that came out of the silence when you least expected it and whacked you over the head. BAM! But his tone was so pure, so beautiful, that it was more like being seduced than bludgeoned or dazzled.

It was totally revolutionary, like an Impressionist in a group of Renaissance painters. And it worked. In fact, it was the perfect counterpoint for the complexity that characterized the playing of many of his peers.

Miles worked his sound relentlessly to create something unlike what any other trumpet player was doing or had done before him.

He somehow knew that bebop would run its course. What he might not have known was that it would be largely up to him to create the new path of jazz.

His sound was totally unique and constantly evolving. But it was his skill as a composer and bandleader that made Miles so great. As leader, he would not tell his band members what to play. Rather, he would present an idea and suggest to them how it might evolve. Then it was up to them.

Because of this style, he attracted some of the best players in the world – names like John Coltrane, Bill Evans, Ron Carter, Cannonball Adderley, and Jo Jones.

On his 1959 album *Kind of Blue*, with many of the world's best players sitting alongside him, he created what most musicologists would argue is the best and most important record in jazz history.

And that was just the beginning.

He was the first jazzer to see what was happening in rock-'n'-roll and embrace it rather than fight it.

He almost singlehandedly created fusion, funk, and what became the roots of hip hop.

His bands became the training ground for many of the best and most important players of the late 20th century. Miles brought kids into his bands, worked them hard, and turned out seasoned pros. The names of Miles alumni are a Who's Who of jazz and rock: Herbie Hancock, Chick Corea, John Mclaughlin, Mike Stern, John Abercrombie, Tony Williams, Jaco Pastorius.

The secret of Miles as a leader was the secret of his approach to music. He created an environment where these often nervous young players could try new things, take chances, create new sounds, and be uniquely themselves. As long as you were taking chances and trying new things, you were OK with him. It was only the "same old same old" that was to be avoided at all costs.

You can judge a great teacher not just by what his pupils do when they are with him, but, more importantly, by what they do when they have left. Miles Davis and his protégés changed the face of music and left us all a lesson we should never forget: Breathe. And listen.

Breathe.

*If you don't own **Kind of Blue** by Miles Davis, you should.*

Ponderables

Who are your favorite musicians? Why? How do they connect with you?

Miles Davis was a master of using space. He was totally comfortable with silence, an unusual characteristic for someone in his business and our society.

Have you ever listened to music and listened to the spaces between the notes rather than the notes?

How about with conversations. Do you ever listen to the spaces as well as the words?

How comfortable are you with space and silence? Do you spend time in silence?

Most people are not very comfortable with either. But it could be argued that a leader's greatest skill is the ability to listen.

And I would argue that to be a great listener, you have to be comfortable with the spaces as well as the sounds.

Oprah Winfrey

The ability to triumph begins with you.
– Oprah Winfrey

One of the good, and bad, aspects of supposed "freedom of speech" is that it removes accountability from the media. Under this concept anyone can say anything, and any network can present anything.

The medium simply has to appeal to the lowest common denominator of society, offer some much-needed money to people to embarrass themselves publicly, and voilà, you have a television show.

The truth is, much of our society is addicted to rubbernecking. We would rather hear bad news than good, are stimulated by violence and humiliation, and are gratified by other people's misfortunes. I am reasonably certain that psychologists would say that indulging in other people's misfortunes is simply a way of aggrandizing our own self-esteem. After all, no matter how bad we feel, the logic goes, "at least we aren't a complete loser like that person."

With a world teetering on self-implosion, as it is, I would like to think that those of us who have some semblance of health, have food and shelter and enough money to buy a TV, would have better things to do all day than revel in the misfortunes of others.

Unfortunately, this is not true.

Jerry Springer, host of the sadly popular TV show of the same name, will go to his grave a wealthy man knowing that he has lied to himself by saying, "But it is what people want to see." He knows that this is just self-justification for achieving fame and wealth by serving up schlock. Shame on you, Mr. Springer. And I will put most of the creators of reality television programs on the list with him.

Thank goodness, there are exceptions. People who have decided to use the unfathomable power of the media, and particularly television, to do something good for the world.

They may not be perfect, but at least they are trying.

One of my heroes has a television show. Count the strikes against her as she started in the world.

Dirt poor. Black. Female. Rural Mississippi, in the 1950s. Parents never married. Left on a farm to be raised by her grandmother. Raped by a cousin at the age of nine. Sexually abused through much of the rest of her childhood.

Her beginning was so bad that they spelled her name wrong on her birth certificate. She was supposed to be named "Orpah," after the biblical character. Instead, she became "Oprah."

How many people do you know whose name is a typo?

She had the daily love and caring of her grandmother, and perhaps only one other thing going for her: she loved to read.

In books she learned about people and worlds that weren't like her own, so she knew there was the possibility of a different life.

In fact, as she tells the story, she was standing on her back porch one day at age three or four while her grandmother was boiling water to wash the clothes. She looked at the scene and knew that somehow, her life would not be like that.

It was not arrogance, it was just a sense of knowing.

We become what we believe. Our thoughts create our reality.

She was reading at age three and reciting Bible verses in front of her church congregation. As she tells it, the women would sit in the front row fanning themselves in the heat and say to her grandmother, "Hattie Mae, I believe that child is gifted." And her grandmother constantly reinforced in the young Oprah that she was talented.

But a gift alone won't get you from the back woods of Mississippi to the top of the world.

A cynic would say Oprah was lucky. And if you believe her definition of luck, that may be accurate: *"Luck is preparation meeting opportunity."*

She left her grandmother's care to live with her mother in a bad area of Milwaukee at age six. It was not a good time. But opportunity came knocking in sixth grade when a teacher who noticed her passion for reading helped her get a scholarship to a better school.

She was prepared. And she never looked back.

She moved to Nashville at 14 to live with her father. He was a strict disciplinarian who helped her focus in order to use her talents and to excel at school. But perhaps the turning point in her life came in the form of a different opportunity: she won the prestigious title of "Miss Fire Prevention Nashville."

Now, not a lot of people can claim that their life changed by being named Miss Fire Prevention. But you see, she was invited to the local radio station to be interviewed. She made such an impression that the station staff asked her if she would like to stay behind after the interview to record her voice so she could hear what she sounded like.

Did she? She had been preparing for this opportunity since she was three.

She blew them away and was given a job reading the news. Around this time her academic excellence and public speaking skills, which she had continued to refine, got her a scholarship to Tennessee State University.

It was quite an achievement. In 1971, not many impoverished, abused black girls were given the opportunity to attend university.

Two years later, she made the move to TV, becoming Nashville's first African-American, first female, and youngest news announcer.

But she had a fatal flaw: she was too human for the news. She cried at the sad stories and refused to stick the camera in the faces of people who had just suffered terrible tragedies. She also had the bad habit of laughing at herself when she made mistakes. Can't do that if you're going to be on TV news.

She moved to Baltimore, where she was teamed up with an older, white male news anchor who was none too happy about sharing the desk with her. Her too human traits and penchant for ad-libbing worked to his advantage, and she was pulled from the news.

As consolation, she was given the co-host spot on a morning news/talk show called "People Are Talking." It did not have great ratings at the time. But it was the only card she had, so she played it. And, as it turns out, it was the perfect format for her style.

As she says, after the first show she knew she had found her calling. *"It was like breathing for the first time,"* she said.

And thus began the career of one of television's most important stars.

Eight years later, she mailed an audition tape to Chicago and won the coveted job as host of the talk show "AM Chicago." At the time, Phil Donahue owned the daytime talk show ratings, but after just one month, he would lose his crown to Oprah forever. And she would never look back.

Quite a ride from a porch in Mississippi watching her grandmother boil water to wash the clothes.

Oprah will tell you that the secret of her success has been her belief in herself.

Supported by a powerful religious faith, and told by her grandmother through her early years that she was gifted, she simply refused to believe in the limited future that society allowed a young black woman in America in the late 20th century.

That belief in herself, coupled with a tremendous work ethic, has kept her going, despite her often public struggles to overcome the demons of her past abuse and her ongoing challenges with her weight.

In fact, it has been her willingness to be herself, flaws and all, that has contributed in no small way to her success.

It takes courage to be a leader.

Today, Oprah is the most powerful woman in the entertainment industry, presiding over a multibillion-dollar multimedia empire.

Her list of industry awards is surpassed only by her seemingly countless humanitarian awards. She has never forgotten her roots.

She is relentless in her efforts to help people improve their lives through her grants and foundations. She is unabashed about wielding the power of her mighty Rolodex for a good cause.

And in perhaps her most important contribution to humanity, she has probably encouraged more people in North America to read books than anyone in history.

Ironic for a television host, isn't it?

Critics will say that *Oprah* is just another variation of the tabloid TV genre that Donahue, and then Jerry Springer, Jenny Jones, Montel Williams, and others, have turned into lowbrow TV.

But I don't agree. While there is plenty of human tragedy on *Oprah*, ultimately the show is a celebration of human perseverance against odds.

Oprah's goal is not to sensationalize. It is to show people that there is a way through their challenges. And she is the poster girl for everything that this represents.

Does she make mistakes on her show? Absolutely.

Is she herself perfect? Absolutely not.

Is she sometimes a shill for blatantly materialistic values? Certainly.

Does the melodrama sometimes go over the top? Maybe.

Does she have an ego? You don't get where she is without one.

But on the other hand …

Has she helped people see possibilities for themselves that they otherwise would not? Absolutely.

In doing so, has she helped people find their way to a better life? You bet.

Has she personally helped people as one of the world's greatest philanthropists? Undoubtedly. Oprah has given away hundreds of millions of dollars and, with that money, has helped hundreds of thousands if not millions of people.

Is she sincerely committed to using her incredible power to make a difference? Unquestionably.

Has she used that power wisely? For the most part.

Oprah is not the second coming. She will be the first to tell you that. But damn, she is living proof to me of what human beings can do if they nurture the talents they are born with, no matter how seemingly meager those talents.

But there are many great philanthropists, great teachers, and socially conscious celebrities out there. So what is the mark of Oprah?

I think it is this: In a society that never stops selling us its idea of perfection, Oprah has taught that none of us, including herself, is perfect. And that that's OK.

Being a leader is not about being perfect. Being a leader is about committing to a never-ending journey of self-improvement.

As Oprah has shown, it matters not whence you came, nor what your particular destination. It matters only that you believe in yourself and are prepared to do whatever it takes to live out your destiny.

As Oprah once said:

> My intention is always for people to see within each show … that you are responsible for your life. That although there may be tragedy in your life, there is always a possibility to triumph. It doesn't matter who you are or where you came from. And that the ability to triumph begins with you. Always.

The ability to triumph begins with you.

There's one to stick on your bathroom mirror.

Ponderables

It's my experience that most workplaces force us to subjugate huge parts of our personalities in order to fit in.

At home we are human. We laugh and we cry. We go see our favorite bands and cheer. We cry at sad movies. We have a few drinks or whatever and dance at parties. If we are lucky, we get silly. We crawl around in the playground or on the floor with our kids. We even sometimes get dirty – ohmygawd!

But in most companies, when we show up for work we leave that side of ourselves behind. Because we are "at work." And at work, all too often, being human is somehow confused with being unprofessional.

Who made that rule?

Small companies are typically the exception to this. They're more spontaneous, more emotional, more fun, and more human. And they get far more out of their people per cubic inch, and far more loyalty, than large corporations.

I have run businesses all my life, and without exception, the secret of the success of these businesses was that we allowed – no, we encouraged – people to be themselves. We expected them to bring their entire selves to work, flaws and all.

This created an environment where our people felt comfortable and safe, an environment that allowed them to do things they never dreamed they could do. It also attracted the very best talent in our industries, because people wanted to work in a company like that.

A leader's behavior sets the tone for an organization. How the leaders act is how the company acts.

One of the many things I love about Oprah is her willingness to be vulnerable. She laughs. She cries. She puts the pounds on and takes them off, sharing her anguish along the way.

By doing this, as a leader, she says, "It's OK to be human," and she gives everyone around her permission to do the same.

How about your behavior? What permissions does it give to those around you? And what behaviors does it encourage?

The Activists

Aung San Suu Kyi

*It is not power that corrupts, but fear. Fear of losing power
corrupts those who wield it, and fear of
the scourge of power corrupts
those who are subject to it.*
– Aung San Suu Kyi

I often wonder how committed and how
courageous I really am.

I think I am pretty committed, say, to writing this
book, and to influencing people's lives with it. I am
also very committed to being the best parent I
possibly can be.

I suppose I am courageous. I am an entrepreneur and
always have been. I also write, play music, and speak
in public, all of which could be considered mildly
courageous acts.

But, as my father was very fond of saying, *"Everything's a matter of proportion."*

Compared with Aung San Suu Kyi, I am in the stands
watching the game.

I first heard of her thanks to the U2 song "Walk On"
from the album *All That You Can't Leave Behind*. The
song is dedicated to her and contains the album's
title line.

For most of us in the West, the concept of being a political prisoner is very foreign. We have freedom of almost every kind – some days too much freedom. So it is difficult to understand someone who believes in something so passionately that they would give up their freedom – their way of life – for it. It is difficult to conceive of the courage it takes to stand up to a military junta, putting your life directly at risk.

Nelson Mandela did, lived to tell about it, and is helping to change the world. Many others have not been so fortunate. And thousands languish to this day in prisons around the world because they dared to disagree with the ruling powers in their country – or in some cases, the ruling powers in foreign countries.

Held against their will, without trial, without legal representation, and usually without communication with the outside world, they die a slow and lonely death.

Aung San Suu Kyi is not exactly one of those. She could fly like a singing bird in an open cage, as Bono describes it. But she chooses not to.

Would you have the courage to make that choice?

Burma, 1947. A father and political activist named General Aung San has successfully led the country's struggle for independence from Britain when he is cut down by assassins' bullets.

His two-year-old daughter is suddenly fatherless, left only with the heroic stories of a leader whom she will never know. But the stories leave a deep imprint.

She is fortunate enough to go to school in India and then in England, get a college degree from Oxford, and see the world firsthand working for the United Nations. But she never forgets the struggle in her homeland and senses that someday she may be needed to pick up where her father left off.

She marries and has children in England. In 1988 she returns to her homeland to care for her dying mother. While she is there, General Ne Win, head of the brutal military government, steps down, leaving an opportunity.

It is her time, and she does what she knows in her heart she is supposed to do.

Along with several other freedom lovers, she begins a powerful pro-democracy movement and a group called the National League for Democracy. She speaks at hundreds of rallies, preaching non-violence in the tradition of Gandhi and Martin Luther King, Jr., fearlessly staring rifles right in the barrel on many occasions. Her peaceful, Buddhist demeanor is loving and kind.

She instantly becomes a national hero. She is reverently referred to as "The Lady."

And that, of course, is exactly the opposite of what any ruling military junta in the world wants. She might as well have painted a target on her chest.

While thousands of others in her democratic party are killed and tortured for standing up for their beliefs, the military leaders are smart enough not to make a martyr of her. So in 1989, Suu Kyi is placed under house arrest. She is not allowed to venture outside her home, and her communication with the outside world is largely cut off.

Her country is renamed Myanmar.

In 1990, an election is held, and her National League for Democracy wins 80% of the parliamentary seats, but the military junta refuses to hand over power. International pressure on the corrupt government intensifies, to no avail.

In the same year, the European Parliament awards Aung San Suu Kyi the Sakharov Prize for Freedom of Thought.

The next year, she wins the Nobel Peace Prize and donates the entire $1.3 million prize to a trust fund for health care for the citizens of her country.

In 1995, she is released from house arrest and told she is free to leave the country. In fact, she is encouraged to leave. The intent is a bit obvious. She knows she will never be allowed back in her homeland if she goes.

She is left with a heart-wrenching choice: go to England to be with her beloved husband and children, whom she has not seen for years, or stay and fight for freedom.

She stays. So deep is her commitment to her people, her country, and to the legacy of her father that she cannot go. Her newfound freedom inside the country proves to be problematic. She rouses the spirit of the people and once again is a threat to the government.

She receives notice that her husband has prostate cancer in England. He is not allowed to visit her, and again, she knows she cannot visit him if she ever wants back into her country.

In 1999, he succumbs to cancer. A thousand people join her at her home to hold a private ceremony in his honor. The government takes their names as they leave. The guests are clearly now on a "watched" list.

Over the next few years she is in and out of house arrest. Then, while she is out of her house in 2003, her convoy is attacked by thugs associated with the ruling militia. In a failed assassination attempt, the attackers beat to death about 100 supporters of the National League for Democracy. Aung San Suu Kyi is returned to house arrest under the pretext of protection, and has not yet emerged.

And so it goes to this day. Only occasionally allowed out of her home, and having next to no communication with the outside world.

As Bono describes it, she understands and lives in "a place that has to be believed to be seen." The place is not Burma. It is far deeper. It is a place called courage.

She will not take up arms, nor allow her supporters to do so. She believes in peace, in cooperation, and in compromise, and lives them every day.

How long will her struggle go on? At what price?

We can only watch, wait, and support her through the UN and human rights groups.

And probably the most important thing any of us can do spiritually for her is never, ever take the freedom we have for granted. Not for a moment.

Ponderables

Lance Armstrong, the seven-time Tour de France champion, was often asked, "Why?" Why would someone subject himself to the torture of The Tour year after year for seven years?

His answer, paraphrased, was, "I love to test myself.
To see how deep and how good I am."

How many of us really know how deep we are, how
good we are?

What are you prepared to give up your life for?
What are you prepared to give up your lifestyle for?

What are you prepared to do to get what you say you
want?

Maybe finding the answers is a journey worth taking.
How you do that is a personal issue.

Aung San Suu Kyi is doing it by sacrificing her freedom, every day of her life.

As a footnote, testosterone has ruled the world for
a few thousand years now and, in the areas of peace
and human rights, the record is not so good.

I say it is time to hand over the reins.

Sir Bob Geldof & Live Aid

*It's really very simple, Governor. When people are hungry
they die. So spare me your politics and tell me
what you need and how you're going
to get it to these people.*
– Sir Bob Geldof

As you have seen, I have tremendous respect for
anyone who stands up for what they believe in.
When they do it for something in which they have
absolutely no personal stake, my respect increases
significantly.

When they do it with the entire world watching,
knowing that if they fail they will be disgraced for
life, they become one of my heroes.

This is the story of one such person.

It is also the story of one of the world's most courageous events, perhaps still the world's greatest freebie. It was moment that saved lives, changed lives,
and altered the very way we think about the world
we live in.

Now, putting on a big event is very stressful. I know
because I have done it most of my adult life. It is
stressful because you only get one chance to do it
right. There is no editing, no opportunity to fix bad

decisions, no going back.

Whatever you have done, however prepared you and the performers are, it's all out there, good or bad, for the audience to see.

At one such event, over 20 years ago, people around the world watched, were touched, were moved to tears, and then to action.

Cynicism is the cancer of society. It is a copout. An excuse for apathy.

In my teens and 20s I thought it was cool to be a cynic. I thought it was a badge of intellectualism. Today I think it is deplorable. Being a cynic is easy. Doing something to make a real difference – now that's hard.

Unfortunately, both cynicism and apathy are often the result of frustration. This frustration often arises from the belief that as one small person out of more than six billion on planet Earth, you really can't do much to make a difference.

But of course, if we all thought and acted like that, things would be much worse than they are.

The Irish statesman Edmund Burke once said, *"Nobody made a greater mistake than he who did nothing because he could only do a little."*

October 1984. The BBC aired an incredibly powerful documentary on the plight of the famine-ravaged people of Ethiopia. Millions of people saw the broadcast, including an Irish punk rocker named Bob Geldof.

Millions of viewers saw this terrible tragedy and presumably at least thought, "Wow, that's sad," and then went about their lives again.

Geldof did not.

At the time, he sang and played guitar in a band called the Boomtown Rats. They had had some success in Europe, with just one song on the top of the international charts: "I Don't Like Mondays." By Bob's own admission, the Rats had already peaked and were on the slope to who knows where.

After that broadcast, Geldof became outraged that people should die of hunger in Africa while food was being thrown away in other parts of the world. "Only in Africa," he thought, "could this kind of tragedy happen and be virtually ignored by the rest of the world."

He decided to do something.

He put a bowl on the kitchen table in his flat, and when his friends came over he asked them to throw in a quid or two for the starving people of Ethiopia.

Hey, every little bit helps.

Then one day he got an idea and called his friend Midge Ure, who had a band called Ultravox. Together they wrote the song "Do They Know It's Christmas?"

They got on the phone and called their pals in the industry – Sting, Bono, George Michael, Paul McCartney, and dozens more. A few weekends later, this collection of many of Europe's top recording artists converged on a studio and recorded their little song.

They rushed it into stores just before Christmas, hoping to raise £70,000. By now the media had picked up on it and the airplay was incessant.

They raised over £12 million.

That drew the attention of America. Lionel Ritchie and Michael Jackson teamed up and wrote a song. Together with Harry Belafonte, Ritchie's manager Ken Kragen, and producer Quincy Jones they pulled together an equally star-studded cast of singers ranging from Ray Charles and Diana Ross to Willie Nelson, Kenny Loggins – and Bob Geldof.

They recorded "We Are the World" and garnered considerably more press coverage than their European counterparts. Launched with great fanfare, its first pressing sold out almost instantly, and the recording went on to raise an estimated $40 million.

By then, Geldof's Band Aid and the American USA for Africa had raised a combined total of around $60 million. Bob was virtually bankrupt at the time. His new career as a fundraiser had put a screeching halt to any hope of resurgence for the Boomtown Rats.

But he couldn't stop. Because by then he realized that he could make a difference. Geldof was about to leave his career as a rocker behind and become the world's highest-profile emissary for famine relief.

His next idea was a concert. Actually it was a telethon cleverly disguised as a concert. But it would be unlike anything before. It would have two huge venues on either side of the Atlantic, on the same day, broadcast to the world.

It would involve all the biggest names in pop music – all of them. But the kicker was that it would all be done for free. Everything. All the money raised would go to the newly established Live Aid fund and the people of Ethiopia.

Now, George Harrison had done the Concert for Bangladesh before and raised some money. Jerry Lewis' telethons for muscular dystrophy were an institution in America. But no one had even imagined a fundraiser on this scale.

Think about this. It's one thing to imagine Geldof phoning up his pals and asking them to take part. It's quite another to imagine a relatively unknown, shaggy, abrasive punk rocker calling the CEOs of the world's largest satellite networks; television networks; phone networks; telecom suppliers; the huge venues and their unions; staging, food, toilet, security, and cleanup suppliers at the two venues; legions of people to man the phones to take donations (there was no Internet); and banks around the world to deal with the money that came in.

Sure, Bob, no problem. We'll get right on that.

He also had to find and bring on board the small pool of incredibly skilled experts it would take to pull off this ridiculous idea, as well as thousands of volunteers, the world's most difficult and demanding rock stars and their handlers, and legions of lawyers. And for the icing on the cake, he wanted British Airways to donate the Concorde for a day so a few people could be at both shows.

What exactly was he thinking?

And let's be clear. He wasn't the Queen or the prime minister, Sir Paul McCartney or Richard Branson, the head of Sony Music or someone equally well empowered and connected.

He was a guitar player and singer in a one-hit punk band.

But Geldof could not be refused. His passion was so intense, his cause so important, that no one with a conscience could say no and walk away. He pushed. He cajoled. He confronted. He demanded. And he did it with a clear conscience, knowing that his cause was life or death for millions of people.

He brought the best people in the world onto his team. His

vision was extraordinarily ambitious: assemble two immense concerts and a global communications network in just a few months, with nearly everything done as a freebie.

But as a leader he did what he needed to do. He made a lot of tough decisions and took a lot of flack for them, and otherwise let the experts do what they were expert at.

Fast forward just a few months to Saturday, July 13, 1985.

Geldof was running on, oh, about two hours' sleep in the last week, and looked and felt like hell.

Talk about being outside your comfort zone! Just a few months before, Geldof was a punk rocker. Now he was the world's foremost expert on famine relief. A man with no experience in broadcasting or fundraising was attempting the largest broadcast concert and charitable experiment ever undertaken.

Between London and Philadelphia, a team consisting mostly of volunteers was going to stage and broadcast an event as complex as a small Olympic Games. While an Olympic Games has many years to plan and build, his thrown together team of volunteers had done so in just a few months.

For most of those months, Geldof had stuck his face and cause in front of every journalist in the world who would listen. Every scribe. Everyone with a camera or tape recorder. Anyone who would help spread the word. Live Aid was in the media in every country of the world.

If it screwed up technically, if no money was raised after all the hype, if it was a bust, there was not a cave deep enough on earth for Geldof to hide in for the rest of his life. He would forever be "that guy who screwed up Live Aid."

To me, that's putting everything on the line. That's courage.

Of course, Live Aid didn't screw up. It was pure magic.

The biggest names in rock music turned out. The music was great, the technical problems minimal, and it actually produced a few of the classic moments in rock history, including the un-forgettable steamy duet of Mick Jagger and Tina Turner.

And people responded. It was estimated that up to two billion people tuned in through the day around the world. Then they phoned in to give – tens of millions of dollars.

The giving did not stop at the emotional singing of "We Are the World" and the raising of Geldof on proud shoulders as the Philadelphia show came to an end. People continued to give at their banks and trust companies over the weeks that followed.

Did it touch people? Geldof tells the story of running into two elderly women in Dublin who were pawning their wedding rings because they were the only things they owned of any value that could be turned into donations.

And in the end an estimated $100 million was raised for the people of Ethiopia on one day.

The cynics, of course, say that much of the money never made it to the people who needed it. Then again, these are the same cynics who sat on their arses while Geldof and his amazing freebie team stayed up night after night without sleep. I dismiss them summarily.

Sadly, there are many corrupt politicians and administrations between Live Aid and the people ravaged by famine. And, indeed, the challenges of Band Aid since the concert have all had to do with getting the money to the people who need it.

Band Aid runs a very efficient machine because it does not have the years of bureaucracy and politics acquired by most large global relief agencies. And to me, only the most cynical would suggest that doing nothing would have been preferable. I am also reasonably confident that the millions of Ethiopians who have been saved would agree with me.

What, ultimately, is the mark of Sir Bob Geldof?

To me it's this. For one day, for an instant in time, he got tens of millions of people around the world to stop being apathetic – to stop being cynical – and to take action. To help people they had never met, in a country they would likely never visit, who could not help themselves.

In doing this he changed the consciousness of several generations. He made us realize that we are all connected. He made us see that that there is a price to pay for turning a blind eye to tragedy. Were it not for the "lucky sperm or egg," any of us reading this book could have been one of the starving in Ethiopia.

In doing all this, Geldof set the stage and raised the bar for every large-scale fundraiser and relief effort that has taken place since. From Farm Aid to Tsunami and Katrina relief, all of them owe their inspiration to an Irishman who started by putting a bowl on his kitchen table.

In making a difference to so many people, Geldof answered a question that most people have asked in frustration at some point in their lives:

"Can one person really make a difference?"

Geldof's answer: "Oh, you betcha!"

> *You can support Bob Geldof and his causes through the Band Aid Charitable Trust or through Make Poverty History (www.makepoverty history.org), his current crusade with Bono to make this generation the one that will put an end to world poverty, starting with Africa.*

Ponderables

I have great respect for the way Bob Geldof ventured into territory about which he knew absolutely nothing, got outside his comfort zone, and made something amazing happen.

Have you ever thought about your comfort zone? Very few, if any of us, is really fearless.

And I am not talking about physical risks, like the nonsense on *Fear Factor*. Fear of death or injury is a natural self-defense mechanism.

I am talking about the more insidious things: fear of being embarrassed, of having no friends, of being alone, of getting fired, of going broke, of getting sick, of losing a loved one ... you get the idea.

Describe your comfort zone.

What things are you most afraid of? What do you do to avoid them? What do you sacrifice by doing so?

On the other hand, what things do you do to stay comfortable – to maintain your lifestyle or habits?

What do you sacrifice by doing so?
What one thing would you never risk?

Are you sure?

And from the legacy of Bob Geldof, one question that I am sure he would ask:

What could you do to make a difference? In your family, your company, your community, the world?

Candy Lightner & MADD

Courage is the price that life exacts for granting peace.
The soul that knows it not knows no
relief from little things.
– Amelia Earhart

One view of life is that it is a series of moments made of choices. The path we choose is simply the path we create from the choices we make.

I have made some choices at various moments in my life that, today, I would make differently were I given the opportunity to recreate my path. I am sure I am not alone in that.

On more than one occasion as a young man, I was out at the pub with friends and chose to drive my car home. No one was ever hurt as a result, but that was either luck or an angel was watching over me.

Today, as the father of a young child, I read in sorrow and anger the stories of people whose lives have been destroyed by someone who should not have been behind the wheel of a car or boat.

This is the completely amazing story of someone who did something about it.

As a leader, I am in awe of this woman and her story. As a parent, I am eternally grateful.

How many of you who are not politicians think you could get the laws changed in your city or town? If you just decided to go out and try to do it, could you succeed? How about across your country? How about around the world?

That's a big task. Politicians spend their careers trying to change laws about which they are personally passionate and often do not succeed.

One woman changed laws that affect every single one of you reading this. And you probably don't know her name: Candy Lightner.

This story began in tragedy in 1980.

Candy's 13-year-old daughter, Cari, was killed by a drunk driver in the middle of the afternoon in California. It was an incident that would have brought many parents' lives to complete collapse.

To add insult to tragedy, the driver had already been charged with several previous counts of impaired driving, had been convicted three times, and had been released on bail just two days earlier after committing a hit and run. For killing young

Cari, he was sentenced to two years in jail, of which he served just 16 months.

An enraged Candy made a vow: *"I promised myself on the day of Cari's death that I would fight to make this needless homicide count for something positive in the years ahead,"* she said.

She gathered a few friends at a steakhouse in Sacramento and formed a group called Mothers Against Drunk Drivers (today "Driving"), better known as MADD.

And then they set out to do something.

At the time, drinking and driving was not just common, it was almost socially acceptable. Everyone drank. "I was drunk" was a legitimate excuse for just about anything. People simply got in their cars after drinking and drove.

At what price?

An astounding 70 people a day were killed in the U.S. by drunk drivers at the time. But no one was doing anything about it.

Candy found countless families who had suffered similar tragedies to hers, and other mothers who were also out to make a change. They had no legal or political experience, which actually may have worked to their advantage, because they simply did not understand the impossibility of what they wanted to do.

You don't just go out and get the laws changed. It is not that simple.

But they were quick studies and smart. They armed themselves with statistics. And maybe most important, their passion was undeniable. They learned how to work the media and very quickly brought their issue to the public eye.

MADD started at the state level, and their passionate plea gained support from their senators and Governor Jerry Brown of California. They got on TV, went before the Senate and House of Representatives, and pleaded their case to receptive ears.

Their point of view was incontestable. They were mothers who had suffered the most unimaginable of losses, so they won their critics over not just with facts but with emotion. Ultimately you were either with them or you didn't care if kids (or anyone) got killed by drunks in cars.

Easy choice.

New, tougher penalties for drinking and driving began to be enacted. Pressure mounted at the state and federal levels to raise the drinking age to 21.

And in perhaps its most potent strike on the public's consciousness, MADD introduced the simple concept of the Designated Driver.

As Candy said, *"If you want to drink, that's your business. But as soon as you drink and get behind the wheel of a car, it becomes my business."*

Now think about how hard it is to coin a phrase and have it become part of mainstream American English. But the concept was intelligent, it demanded accountability of people, and it provided a great solution to those who were certainly not going to stop partying because some woman had lost her child to an idiot.

"Designated Driver" became part of the lexicon.

A year after the organization began, there were ten MADD chapters across the United States. The following year, there were more than 70. All were volunteer, and all started by word of mouth. The Barnes Bill, which sought to raise the national drinking age to 21, struck a public chord. Though it had been ignored a year earlier, the bill, with the exposure of MADD behind it, now garnered unprecedented support and was passed. And soon after, MADD successfully got the legal limit set at .8 for blood alcohol while driving.

Today there are 600 MADD chapters around the world, predominantly in North America. More important, it is estimated that since the inception of MADD in 1980, drunk-driving fatalities in the U.S. have decreased by 43%.

Starting out as a group of bereaved mothers at a California steakhouse, MADD has changed laws at every level. It has created new phrases and images and integrated them into the mainstream. And, most significantly, MADD has helped change how society views the responsibility required if a person is going to drink alcohol.

MADD is one of the few grassroots organizations in our culture that have successfully changed the public's consciousness and conscience. Every one of us who drinks alcohol thinks and acts differently about drinking and driving than we did 25 years ago.

Cari Lightner's death was a wasteful and terrible tragedy. But Candy can indeed live with the knowledge that her daughter's life made a difference.

MADD has helped save the lives of hundreds of thousands of people, changed the lives of hundreds of millions of others, and prevented many parents from suffering the grief that Candy did.

To Candy Lightner and her colleagues, I tip my hat, touch my heart, and say thanks for your powerful leadership that turned tragedy into triumph.

Ponderables

It's useful to think back through our lives and remember the big moments of decision and the choices we made. It is particularly important, for the sake of this discussion, to consider the bad moments – the loss of a loved one, an accident, the breakup of a relationship, the loss of a job.

What were those moments for you?

What choices did you make at the time?

Did you decide to do anything different personally or professionally?

What were the results? Did anything actually change if you wanted it to change?

What would have been different if you had made other choices at the time?

There is a famous saying that goes: "Fool me once, shame on you. Fool me twice, shame on me."

I love to ask myself whether I have learned from my mistakes and my tragedies, or whether I am going to see them all again in a different form before I die to make sure I "got it."

Many people have said some version of the phrase, "It's not what happens to you, it's what you do about it."

There's no doubt in my mind that commitment in a leader is the ability to keep going even when life throws the worst at you.

It's easy to lead when everything is going well. Real leaders prove themselves when things aren't.

Florence Nightingale

I think one's feelings waste themselves in words;
they ought all to be distilled into actions
which bring results.
– Florence Nightingale

Most of us spend our lives trying to avoid hospitals, for obvious reasons. But it is hard to get through life without having to go there more than once.

Sadly, the hospital experience varies widely around the world, depending on where you are, whom you know, and how much money you have. Maybe Starbucks could give some global advice on creating a great and consistent customer experience at hospitals.

The quality of your doctor(s) will ultimately have a powerful impact on the outcome of any treatment. But the quality of your experience at the hospital is much more deeply impacted by the nurses to whom you trust your care and recuperation.

Most of us have nurse stories – bad and good. I wish the bad nurses would change careers.

But the good ones, the angels of mercy! The ones who can make you feel good even when everything in your body hurts. Those nurses should be among the most exalted members of society.

Nursing is a tough job. Nurses are not particularly well paid. Most of them work shifts, which wreaks havoc with their families. Some of them put up with doctors whose bedside manner and leadership skills are abysmal at best. Yet they soldier on.

A nurse changed my life. In fact, a nurse may well have created my life.

My father was badly injured in World War II. His left leg was crushed at the thigh. Doctors in his field camp were going to amputate at the hip, but a nurse insisted that she could help save the leg, and save it they did.

That decision changed his life. What if he had lived the rest of his life with one leg, back when prosthetics were primitive? Would he have been at the party where he met my mother? Would he have been less employable and therefore on a different career path? Would he have played catch with me on the street as I grew up?

Either way, my family and I owe our thanks not only to that nurse, but also to Florence Nightingale, the mother of modern nursing. It was she who forged the path that allowed that wartime field nurse to speak up and be heard.

Some leaders' lives begin with nothing, and their journey is about creating success against the odds. Many of the stories in this book chronicle the journeys of people like that whose courage overcomes.

It is an entirely different and perhaps less common story to be born of wealth and to sacrifice it all to go out into the world and make a difference.

Florence Nightingale was one of those stories. She was born in 1820, not coincidentally, in Florence, Italy, into a wealthy English family. The path for a woman of her social station then was pretty much predetermined: go to good schools, get married, have children, be seen and not heard. It was a path of security and predictability.

But Florence saw her wealthy family's life as idle and sheltered, and she rebelled against it almost from the beginning. Her prodigious intelligence and strong will were taking her somewhere completely different, though she did not at first know where that was.

When she was 17, she found out. God – or whatever you want to call Florence's Higher Power – spoke to her and pointed her in the direction of nursing. It was the first of four times in her life that she would be spoken to in this way.

Nursing at the time was a lowly profession, filled mostly by lower-class women who couldn't find employment anywhere else. It was badly organized and only minimally respected. For a woman of her class and intelligence to have anything to do with it was socially preposterous.

All the more reason for it to be her calling, as far as Florence was concerned.

She was particularly appalled with the conditions of care for the legions of poor and disadvantaged. At age 25 she officially made nursing her life calling, having rejected more than one proposal of marriage and the notion of family.

When the Crimean War broke out in 1854, she organized a party of 38 nurses to travel to the front lines. Medical conditions were atrocious and only got worse as growing numbers of wounded were brought in.

Sadly, the lack of decent hospital conditions was largely driven by the British class system. The wealthy did not serve in the army, or if they did, they were officers and received special treatment. The rank and file were from the lower classes, whose lives were deemed expendable. Spending money and resources for clean facilities and proper care for these lower-class types was just not that important.

As was so often the case, Florence's first task was to convince the doctors to take her and her team seriously. Fortunately, her intellect and her will were prepared for the task. In no time, she and her ragtag team turned conditions around, forced the creation by the government of a Sanitary Commission, and cut the mortality rate by an astounding two-thirds.

When she returned home to England at the end of the war, she was adored by the soldiers for whom she had cared and fought. She became a national hero, earning the nickname "the Lady with the Lamp" because of the Grecian lamp she carried with her when she cared for the injured at night.

The adoration that the common soldier held for Florence was hard-earned and well-deserved. Florence's commitment had been incredible. In addition to lighting her on her nightly rounds, her lamp also allowed her to work late on paperwork, maintaining meticulous medical records for the hospital and writing personal letters to the families of all those soldiers who died.

But she did not want adulation. Nor did she see herself as just a personal caregiver. Her role was much larger. She was a reformer. She had been given gifts, and she would use them to change medical care forever.

Using her considerable influence and persuasion, she took her cause right to Queen Victoria. Through pressure and the brilliant presentation of facts and arguments, she ultimately drove a complete overhaul of the British army's medical system, the results of which had a huge impact on patient care both on the battlefield and at home.

She also attacked the lack of training and standards for

professional nursing. A fund started in her name received tremendous public support and provided the money needed to establish the Nightingale Nursing School in London. Its goal was to improve training in the skills required to be a modern nurse.

Tragically, Florence returned from the Crimea very ill. Struck by what many believe to be a form of today's chronic fatigue syndrome, she withdrew to her room, where she would spend most of the many years that remained in her life.

She continued to direct her efforts to reforming the medical system, writing several books and a 1,000-page report that ultimately helped overhaul the system yet again.

She became an adviser to the American government on treating the wounded and in 1901 became the first woman to receive the Victorian Medal of Honour.

She died in her bed in 1910 at age 90.

Warren Buffet unknowingly summed up the mark of Florence Nightingale when he said: *"Someone is sitting in the shade today because someone planted a tree a long time ago."*

Florence could have chosen the easy path in her story. It was the card she was dealt at birth – money, comfort, security.

Instead, she chose to plant a seed.

My father, my family, and millions of others like us, were allowed to sit in the shade because of that decision.

Ponderables

Here are a few of the questions that the story of Florence Nightingale makes me ask myself:

What are my personal assets? Not my financial assets, but my talents?

What do I do with those assets to plant a tree for other people?

How much of my life is a result of the expectations and circumstances of my childhood?

What is the seed that I am planting?

Who do I hope will one day sit in the shade of the tree I planted, and what benefit will they derive?

Maria Montessori

The greatest sign of success for a teacher ...
is to be able to say, "The children are
now working as if I did not exist."
– Maria Montessori

I remember this of grade school history: my teachers took the entire course of human events – the greatest triumphs and the worst defeats – and made them an incredibly boring exercise in memorization.

They stood at the front of the class and blah-blah-blahed on and on while the class daydreamed. Tests were a simple exercise in memorization. "In 1492, Columbus sailed the ocean blue." Zzzzzzzzzzzz.

This was more than just a few years ago, so we had television sets in a few classes, but no computers. A teaching aid was a pull-down chart.

I remember to this day a teacher of medieval British history who brought a musket – a very old rifle – to class and passed it around so we could touch it and smell it. His gun was hundreds of years old. I can still visualize it, 40 years later. Of all the history classes, I recall only that one.

What I learned that day is that it is our imagination that captures and keeps our attention when we learn, not our intellect. And capturing and keeping attention is best done using more than one of our senses.

As soon as I touched that musket, I felt like I was touching history. At that point, it ceased to be an exercise in memorizing dates and began to be a voyage through the past.

What that history teacher had done was simply to demonstrate something that a very bright Italian woman had figured out much earlier in the century.

Italy, 1870. A woman's opportunities were severely limited.

Women "belonged" to their fathers, husbands, brothers, and uncles, and their future was determined by them and by the all-male clergy of the Roman Catholic Church.

Women were not allowed a public education, a bank account, ownership of property, or a vote.

It was into this male-dominated world that young Maria Montessori was born.

Hers was an educated but not wealthy family, one that had never strayed from the social norm. Their daughter, however, was not someone for whom such norms held much sway. She was fascinated by science and was very good at it, and, in 1894, defied her patriarchal society by becoming the first female physician in Italy.

The males who ran the medical profession did not know what to do with this strong-willed and academically excellent young woman. So she was given the task of caring for – educating – those whom society had deemed "mentally retarded" and "impossible to educate."

She was given a psychiatric position at the University of Rome. There she began exhaustive studies into how children learn. She became convinced that they could learn from their environment, thereby teaching themselves, a theory that totally contradicted the accepted practice of teaching by lecture.

Montessori set out to change the traditional relationship of active teacher and passive student. She believed that interactive environments involving games, exploration, and many tactile and exploratory materials would keep children's interest and attention. The teacher's role became more that of facilitator than lecturer – intervening to help individual children when needed, at the time when they specifically needed it.

Her new ideas had considerable success. Even so-called retarded children flourished in her learning environments.

In 1907 she left the academic world to open a *casa dei bambini*, or "children's house," in a slum outside Rome.

There she took in young children who had been written off because of the impact of the horrible poverty in which they were raised. Once again, in these classrooms where they explored, interacted, and developed at their individual pace, the results were impressive.

She gave them physical objects to touch and manipulate in order to engage all of their senses. They were physically active, rather than simply sitting in a chair listening. They helped each other learn as well as learning on their own. They used and made sounds rather than keeping quiet all the time.

With all of their senses engaged, rather than simply their eyes and ears, the students' learning was astonishing. In fact, even Montessori was surprised. Children were reading and adding multi-digit numbers at ages four and five.

Her success was so significant that she was soon asked to take her methods to other countries. She traveled Europe, Africa, India, Sri Lanka, and ultimately America, helping teachers redesign the way they taught and the way their students learned.

In 1922, while serving a post as a government Inspector of Schools, she was forced to leave Italy because of her staunch opposition to Mussolini's fascism.

She continued to travel the world, spreading her methods through the remainder of her adult life, and was nominated for the Nobel Peace Prize three times. She died in Holland in 1952.

Today, thousands of schools around the world carry the name or accreditation "Montessori" and continue Maria's work of transforming the classroom into a place where all children have a chance to flourish, regardless of their learning ability or financial capabilities.

What is Maria Montessori's mark, and what can we learn from it today?

She gave us some of the keys to improving how we teach and learn. We control our future because we control how and what we and our children learn. So by giving us keys to learning, Montessori gave us important keys to our future.

Will we be wise enough to use them?

The good news is that her methods continue through Montessori schools. Children lucky enough to be part of these get a tremendous head start on their education. My son learned more in three months at a Montessori school last year than in eight months at his public school.

The bad news is that this has not permeated the education system much past the very early years. The kids are more bored than ever, the schools are generations behind in technology, there are metal detectors at the doors of high schools, and college professors are, for the most part, still just giving lectures. Nothing there has changed since ancient Greece.

And when we finish school, things don't get much better.

I believe that adults are no more disposed to sit passively in a conference room for eight hours than children are in a classroom. I have produced thousands of conferences in my life and am a professional speaker. It never ceases to amaze me that corporations – even the good, the wealthy, and the sophisticated ones – still focus 80 to 90 percent of a conference on people sitting in seats with someone talking at the front.

Then, ironically, they spend tens or hundreds of thousands of dollars with production companies making videos and skits and hiring celebrities to wake people up. What's wrong with this picture folks?

In college, you get to talk because you are a subject expert. In the corporate world, you get to talk from the stage not because you are a good speaker, but because of your title or job. The blackboard has been replaced with PowerPoint presentations, most of which contain word slides or charts that no one can see past the front few rows, even if they wanted to.

Why would adults – smart, eager, ambitious, competitive, active adults – find this any more stimulating than their kids would – kids who are skipping their classes because their teachers are so boring?

The question is, when are we going to be wise enough to fix this mess by using the keys that Maria Montessori gave us?

Ponderables

In the 50 or so years since I was born, a lot has changed. That is the understatement of my life.

Today, television screens come in endless shapes and sizes and are everywhere: on cell phones, on seat backs in cars and planes, on portable DVD players, in every room of the house, in sports stadiums, in malls and airports, and in large public squares. We can put anything we want onto those TVs – photos, video images, animation, music, narratives – any media. And, thanks to the Internet, with a handy keyboard or mouse and a connection we can find answers to virtually any question we want.

Despite this, today, for the most part, teachers still stand at the front talking and using the blackboard, and occasionally students have to answer questions.

The system needs changing. We all know it. The teachers are behind. The technology is behind. The teaching methods and curriculum are behind. And the students are bored.

No wonder.

It's no one's fault. That's just the way it is.

Maria Montessori figured out the answer. But are we paying attention?

How do you learn best? Reading, listening, watching, all of the above?

How much of your life do you spend learning new things?

How much of your life do you spend sharing your knowledge and expertise?

Rosa Parks

I have learned over the years that when one's mind is made up, this diminishes fear; knowing what must be done does away with fear.

– Rosa Parks

Ever had one of those days where you've just had enough?

Most of us have days like this. We're tired, stressed, sick, emotionally hurting. Whatever the reason.

It is funny how often a simple request or incident can set you off. That something, and how you respond on any particular day, can change your life forever.

The incident may be something that happens to you all the time and bothers you, but that you do nothing about – something your spouse says, your boss does, or your kids don't do.

Often it's something that happens to you all the time. And one day, instead of letting it all roll off your back, you respond.

You get up and walk away. You say something when you have always been quiet before. You yell. Or you cry. Or you laugh. Or you strike back. Hopefully you do not go postal.

Whatever you do, it is not how you have ever re-sponded before and not what anyone else expects. And sometimes, as a result, the dominoes start to fall, and life is never the same again.

Heroes come in all colors, shapes, and sizes. Very few of them show up in times of trouble wearing a mask, a cape, and boots or riding a white horse.

In real life, heroes don't do the big, miraculous things they do in movies and comics – throwing meteors and bombs off into space, fixing broken railway tracks or dams with their bare hands, or extinguishing fires with their superbreath.

In real life, heroes do small things. Like saving people's lives when they can. Standing up for the weak and oppressed.

Or just saying "no" when they must.

Little things, when put together, become big things. Put a bunch of them together and you change the world.

Alabama, 1955. Being an African American – a "Negro" – was not a life you would have chosen if you lived there. Life was ruled by fear. The Ku Klux Klan was everywhere, looking for blacks to step out of line so they could vent their fear and anger on them.

In Montgomery, the bus system was segregated by law, like everything else. The rules were clear: blacks sat at the back, whites at the front. If the black section was full, any other blacks who got on the bus weren't allowed to sit in the front. But if the white section was full, the blacks at the back were expected to give up their seat for them.

The dividing line between the two sections was completely portable – a simple card that the driver put on a row of seats depending on how busy the bus was. If the white section filled up, he just moved the card back and the black people in that row were supposed to give up their seats and stand.

Simple game. Like fixed gambling tables. The house always wins, no matter what.

Just to make the game more fun, blacks had to enter through the front doors to pay, then get off and re-enter through the back doors to sit. The drivers' favorite trick was to drive off as they were walking between the doors. What fun!

There was just one tiny flaw in the game. Black riders account-ed for 66% of the passengers in Montgomery. Without them, the transit system would go bankrupt.

It was a flaw looking for a sledgehammer to bust it open.

Enter the sledgehammer, a 42-year-old tailor's assistant named Rosa Parks. Quiet. Humble. Self-confident. She was president of the Montgomery National Association for the Advancement of Colored People. Never caused any trouble. Just led a quiet, subservient black person's life in Alabama in the 1950s.

Until December 1, 1955. After a long day at work, she boarded a bus and sat in the first colored row. Nothing unusual, until the driver came along, moved the dividing sign to the row behind her, and asked the four blacks in her row to stand up so the incoming whites could sit.

Three got up and stood. Rosa sat.

The driver asked her to get up. Calmly she replied, "No."

"Pardon me, ma'am?"

"No, I will not."

She knew the consequences, but as she said later, *"I had had enough. I knew it was the very last time I would ever ride in humiliation like that."*

Little did she know.

Rosa was arrested and charged $10 plus $4 court costs. A lawyer friend posted her bail – Rosa didn't have that kind of money. And word hit the street like a tsunami.

Meetings were held. A young local pastor named Dr. Martin Luther King, Jr., got involved. And the next day 35,000 handbills were distributed to black schools asking children and their parents to stay off the bus.

This is what it said:

> We are ... asking every Negro to stay off the buses
> Monday in protest of the arrest and trial ... You can
> afford to stay out of school for one day. If you work,
> take a cab or walk. But please, children and grown-
> ups, don't ride the bus at all on Monday. Please stay
> off the buses Monday.

No threats, no incitements.

Just a simple request.

That Monday, the black community of Montgomery walked or drove to work. They boycotted the bus system – 66% of the city's transit customers. BAM! Them smart white folks didn't see that one coming!

The boycott lasted one year, until the financial consequences to the city were so severe that they rescinded the bus segregation laws.

It was the spark that ignited the fire that changed the racial tone of America, with Dr. King as its leader. Sometimes even a small spark can start a large fire. And this fire was destined to burn for generations.

Rosa's life was in such danger that she was forced to move to Detroit, where she lived the rest of her life. It was not her intent to become a symbol, but she became one – a symbol to people that anyone could stand up for what they believed, particularly in America.

When she died in 2005, at age 92, Rosa Parks became the first woman, the first non-government official, and the second African American to be laid to rest in honor in the U.S. Capitol Rotunda. The funeral of this tailor's assistant was attended by some of the most important people in America, and the world.

Chaos theory suggests that when a butterfly flaps its wings, the impact, however subtle, is felt right around the world.

All of our lives are a series of moments. In those moments we make decisions. With those decisions we flap our wings.

Rosa Parks made her mark with a simple act, and in flapping her wings, she changed the world.

And every one of us has the power to do exactly the same.

Ponderables

What are the three most significant decisions you have made in your life?

What was the impact of those decisions?

What are the three most significant decisions in your life you wish you had made differently?

Sir Winston Churchill

*How old would you be if you didn't
know how old you are?*
– Satchel Paige

I don't cover a lot of political figures in **The Mark
of a Leader**, but this is one of the most important
leadership stories of the 20th century. One could
argue that none of us would have the freedoms we
enjoy without this abrasive, cigar-smoking, hard-
drinking British leader. And any good book on leadership needs at least one story about someone with
visible vices.

Churchill would never make it in politics today –
he would eschew political correctness with a
vengeance. One of my favorite Churchill quotes
comes from this encounter with Lady Astor that
speaks volumes about his personality:

Lady Astor: *Winston, if I were your wife I'd put poison
in your coffee.*
Winston: *Nancy, if I were your husband, I'd
drink it.*

Churchill was a master of the sound bite at a time
when radio and film were just taking off. He was
controversial. He projected fearlessness. He inherited
a big problem – a world-at-risk problem –

and he just got on and dealt with it.

He was at once brilliant and flawed, visionary and very traditional, a master statesman and combative solider.

He was many things and many paradoxes. And here is a sampling of them all.

Our society has a fascination with youth. It drives me crazy. If you believe the media, we're all washed up sometime around age 40. Perhaps it is the media trying to appeal to the elusive youth market and their savings. Or perhaps it is just a sign of our times – tight abs sell more ads. But a fast glance down a magazine rack shows an almost terrifying preoccupation with youth.

Fortunately, not everyone believes that youth is everything.

England, 1939. A 65-year-old career soldier and politician named Winston Churchill had been banished to the back benches of Parliament.

He was an ambitious man driven to live up to the expectations of a demanding and successful father. He was given the best of schooling and a comfortable life, but not what he really craved – love from his father.

Winston believed that he was on earth for some great purpose. Not only had he not yet found it in the 1930s, his career had been marred by as many failures as triumphs.

During World War I, as Lord of the Admiralty, he had led Britain into several disastrous battles and was removed from his post in disgrace.

He had flipped between the Conservative and Liberal parties in Parliament and had been equally belligerent, outspoken, and unpopular to many in each.

By the early 1930s, his political career seemed a thing of the past, and he resigned himself to writing his memoirs and history books to earn a living.

Then a research trip to Germany in 1932 brought him face to face with the rising Nazi youth movement. The rest of the world believed that the threat from Germany had been quelled after World War I. But Churchill saw in Germany the roots of a whole new power even more dangerous than the first.

His warrior instincts were aroused. He returned to England and began what would turn into many years of warning his countrymen of the impending threat.

His warnings were generally met with disbelief. Most of the world believed Germany would stay true to the agreements made after its defeat in World War I.

Prime Minister Chamberlain himself met several times with Hitler and returned convinced that he was a man of honor.

And then one day Churchill was proven right. Hitler began his march across Europe, starting with Austria, and one by one countries fell in his path. When France finally fell, British Prime Minister Chamberlain again suggested meeting with Hitler to discuss terms of a surrender or accord.

Churchill would not hear of it. He said the world needed someone to stand up to Hitler and stop him.

They needed a leader. And that leader was Winston Churchill.

In 1940, in an unprecedented moment, the then disgraced Chamberlain stepped aside and Winston Churchill was made prime minister without an election. Like so many great leaders, he inherited a problem that his predecessor had allowed to fester and grow.

Churchill knew that Britain would be the last major defensive post in Western Europe that could stand up to Hitler's attack. If England fell, the whole face of the earth would change. He knew that the weight of the free world was on his shoulders, and that he must rally his countrymen to hold back the German attack and ultimately lead a victorious offensive.

Like all great leaders, he knew what buttons to push with his people to rally them.

Using his skills as a linguist and orator, and his burning passion for England and for the cause of freedom, he focused on rallying his country's pride. In his first speech as PM, his rhetorical skills were in high gear:

> *I would say to the House, as I said to those who have joined this government: I have nothing to offer but blood, toil, tears, and sweat. We have before us an ordeal of the most grievous kind. We have before us many, many long months of struggle and of suffering.*
>
> *You ask, what is our policy? I can say: It is to wage war, by sea, land, and air, with all our might and with all the strength that God can give us; to wage war against a monstrous tyranny never surpassed in the dark, lamentable catalogue of human crime.*
> *That is our policy.*
>
> *You ask, what is our aim? I can answer in one word: It is victory, victory at all costs, victory in spite of all terror, victory, however long and hard the road may be; for without victory, there is no survival.*
>
> *Let that be realised; no survival for the British Empire, no survival for all that the British Empire has stood for, no survival for the urge and impulse of the ages, that mankind will move forward towards its goal. But I take up my task with buoyancy and hope.*
>
> *I feel sure that our cause will not be suffered to fail among men. At this time I feel entitled to claim the aid of all, and I say, "Come then, let us go forward together with our united strength."*

That speech made clear the vision, the terms, and the path for the future.

His eloquence continued. This is an excerpt from his famous June 1940 speech, often referred to as the "fight on the beaches" speech. Notice the use of short, repetitive phrases to create drama:

> *We shall go on to the end, we shall fight in France, we shall fight on the seas and oceans, we shall fight with growing confidence and growing strength in the air, we shall defend our Island, whatever the cost may be, we shall fight on the beaches, we shall fight on the landing grounds, we shall fight in the fields and in the streets, we shall fight in the hills; we shall never surrender, and even if, which I do not for a moment believe, this Island or a large part of it were subjugated and starving, then our Empire beyond the seas, armed and guarded by the British Fleet, would carry on the struggle, until, in God's good time, the New World, with all its power and might, steps forth to the rescue and the liberation of the old.*

As the clash between Britain and Germany grew closer, Churchill put the stakes of victory on the line for his countrymen even more clearly:

> *I expect that the Battle of Britain is about to begin. Upon this battle depends the survival of Christian civilization. Upon it depends our own British life, and the long continuity of our institutions and our Empire. The whole fury and might of the enemy must very soon be turned on us.*

Hitler knows that he will have to break us in this Island or lose the war. If we can stand up to him, all Europe may be free and the life of the world may move forward into broad, sunlit uplands.

But if we fail, then the whole world, including the United States, including all that we have known and cared for, will sink into the abyss of a new Dark Age made more sinister, and perhaps more protracted, by the lights of perverted science.

Let us therefore brace ourselves to our duties, and so bear ourselves that, if the British Empire and its Commonwealth last for a thousand years, men will still say, "This was their finest hour."

Across the country, glued to their radios, the people of England instantly understood the job ahead, the stakes, the style, the enemy, and the outcomes of failure or victory. There was no doubt about exactly what had to be done, no debate about whether it would happen. There was just action.

Through the rest of the war, as Churchill became the pivot around which the Allied forces rallied, he continued honing the power of his passionate rhetoric.

There was this classic excerpt after Britain finally secured a land victory against Rommel in North Africa:

This is not the end. It is not even the beginning of the end. But it is, perhaps, the end of the beginning.

And look at this challenge he threw at Hitler in 1941:

> We will have no truce or parley with you, or the grisly
> gang who work your wicked will. You do your worst
> – and we will do our best.

Churchill was the voice of the Allied troops. He befriended
America's president Franklin D. Roosevelt and Russia's Joseph
Stalin to bring them into the battle.

And this is the way he described the enemy in his speech to the
Canadian Parliament in 1941:

> There shall be no halting, or half measures, there shall be
> no compromise, or parley. These gangs of bandits have
> sought to darken the light of the world; have sought to
> stand between the common people of all the lands and
> their march forward into their inheritance. They shall
> themselves be cast into the pit of death and shame, and
> only when the earth has been cleansed and purged of
> their crimes and their villainy shall we turn from the task
> which they have forced upon us, a task which we were
> reluctant to undertake, but which we shall now most
> faithfully and punctiliously discharge.

Churchill's passionate rhetoric, his brilliant command of the
English language, his stubborn refusal to even consider surrender, and his keen strategic and diplomatic intelligence
ultimately succeeded in rallying the Allied forces.

The final result of his tireless leadership was, of course, victory.

This was what he said to Britain upon the news of Hitler's defeat.

God bless you all. This is your victory! It is the victory of the cause of freedom in every land. In all our long history we have never seen a greater day than this. Everyone, man or woman, has done their best. Everyone has tried. Neither the long years, nor the dangers, nor the fierce attacks of the enemy, have in any way weakened the independent resolve of the British nation.
God bless you all.

Churchill's mark was helping save the world from Hitler. And we owe him, and everyone who risked and lost their lives, for that. As he said himself;

Never in the field of human conflict was so much owed by so many to so few.

But for those of us who may not have saving the world in our destiny, what is the mark that Churchill left from which we can all learn?

There are three for me.

First, commitment. His career was far from stellar, his life far from happy. He suffered perhaps the greatest tragedy a parent can – losing a child. He had at least as many failures as successes. He suffered long and deep bouts of depression. But he never gave up.

This is a famous excerpt from a speech he gave at Harrow

School in 1941, in which he offered students this advice from what the war had taught him:

> *Never give in, never give in, never, never, never, never*
> *– in nothing, great or small, large or petty – never give in*
> *except to convictions of honor and good sense. Never*
> *yield to force; never yield to the apparently overwhelming*
> *might of the enemy.*

Second, his work ethic. He was a tireless worker. Even in his late 70s he would keep his staff up working until the wee hours of the morning.

One of the world's greatest orators, he had a lisp, which simply drove him to work harder at refining his writing and speaking skills.

Churchill spent one hour writing and learning every minute of his speeches. He was a great orator not only because of a gift, but because he worked so hard at it. For those of you who believe that a few PowerPoint charts are all you need, Mr. Churchill would have another opinion.

Third, and most important of all, passion. For that was what stirred the soul of Britain and the Allied forces.

Churchill showed that passion has no limit and knows no age. At age 65 he hadn't even begun the most important part of his career. His passion was just being ignited to do something really great with his life.

In a society that worships youth, I find that a refreshing

thought. And it is the first thought I am going to have when I wake up on my 65th birthday.

Thank you, Mr. Churchill, for the freedom we all know. And for those great lessons.

Ponderables

In traditional cultures, the elders are those who lead the tribe with their wisdom gained from experience. Today a lot of 25-year-olds armed with MBAs believe they can run large corporations. Only one in a million actually can, because they lack the experience and wisdom.

Today, at least in urban centers, we are led to believe that if we are not retired at 65, we have failed. And how many people do you know who retired at 65 and were dead within a year or two? The golf course just didn't have the appeal when they got there that it did in their imagination. And there was no one to play with!

Today, with proper care and a bit of good luck, there is every expectation that we will live to 100. What we all do in the last quarter of our lives will have a huge impact on the world.

If we can channel the collective wisdom and experience of hundreds of millions of people, it can be a huge force for change.

My hat goes off to the legions of people over 65, 70, 75, and even 80 who have not gone to the golf course but instead are still active in the workforce, active in charities, active in their communities. Just plain active!

What is your plan for Act Four of your life – those years between 75 and 100?

THE MARK OF A LEADER

The Brave Souls

Helen Keller
& Anne Sullivan

When one door closes, another door opens.
But we so often look so long and so regretfully
upon the closed door that we do not see
the ones which open for us.

– Helen Keller

In her great song "Big Yellow Taxi," Joni Mitchell sings the famous line, *"Don't it always seem to go, that you don't know what you've got till it's gone?"*

As my experience in life has grown, so has my understanding of this profound thought.

Joni wrote the song about the environment and the proliferation of parking lots across the world. But her words apply to virtually every aspect of our lives. Sadly, sometimes we have to not have something before we appreciate having it.

I am one of the lucky ones – touch wood. I was born with my five senses all intact and functioning – ditto for my motor skills – so I have been able to lead a pretty independent life.

As I get older, I appreciate my good fortune more and more each day.

Not everyone has been as lucky as I – or perhaps you – have been. Some people are born without one or more of their five senses. Others lose them to disease, accident, or age.

This is the story of one woman who lost her sight and hearing, and of another woman who lost her sight and then partially recovered it.

Two women, each to a different degree vulnerable in a world designed for people with all their senses and motor skills functioning. Two women who found each other, helped each other, and changed the world for millions who followed them.

They were an unlikely team.

Alabama, 1882. At that time in the south there were no rural hospitals. If you got really sick, you were likely to die from your ailment before the doctors in the city could figure out what was wrong with you.

If your name was Helen Keller, an otherwise healthy little girl just shy of your second birthday, the card that fate would deal you would not be death. It would be darkness. And its evil partner, silence.

Imagine if, one day, you could no longer see or hear. Close your eyes and cover your ears for, say, five minutes. Nothing coming in except what you can feel on your skin and taste buds.

If it happened to you for real, you'd probably do what young Helen did. You'd vent your unimaginable frustration with fits and tantrums – screaming at the unseen bars with which you were imprisoned, begging to be set free. To no avail.

Relatives thought her a monster who would never fit into civilized society. As was typical of the day, they thought she should be institutionalized. If you were afflicted like Helen in the 1880s in Alabama, the solution was not to help you – it was to take you out of society. Out of sight, out of mind.

Fortunately, she had someone in her corner. Had she not, we would never have come to know her name.

While she could not be healed, one doctor saw the potential in her abilities and sought special help. He believed she could improve and lead a satisfying life. She simply needed a hero to help her.

He didn't ride in on a white horse. He wasn't a doctor. But he came as her hero all the same.

His name was Bell – Alexander Graham Bell. The man behind the telephone. Bell's own life had been changed by the deafness of his beloved wife, Mabel. He had turned his life's work and genius to the advancement of those without hearing. He saw hope in young Helen's predicament and recommended an unusual pairing. He would team Helen with a young woman named Anne Sullivan.

Helen needed someone who could understand her plight – who would be caring and patient.

The Teacher, as Anne would become known, could do this from firsthand experience. She too had lost her sight at a young age. Through two miracle operations, she had regained enough sight to be able to read for short periods.

The nearly blind leading the blind and deaf. An unusual pair.

Anne's task was to teach Helen to communicate and, in so doing, teach her the lessons of friendship, caring, and trust.

Helen's task, though she didn't know it at first, was to be a friend and to give Anne her life's work and meaning.

It was slow and arduous. Close your eyes again and imagine how you would teach someone who could neither see nor hear you. Where would you start?

Finger spelling was the solution: associating letters with objects. Teaching took place every day.

After a month, a breakthrough occurred. As Anne pumped water over Helen's hand, Helen spelled "water" with her free hand.

As she reminisced of this life-changing event:

> *I stood still, my whole attention fixed upon the motions of her fingers. Suddenly I felt a misty consciousness as of something forgotten, a thrill of returning thought, and somehow the mystery of language was revealed to me.*

That was only the beginning.

Her capacity to gain knowledge was astounding. Helen soon learned to read, beginning with raised letters and Braille, writing on both a traditional and a Braille typewriter.

Braille is significantly more complex than the Roman alphabet. Instead of learning 26 letters, she had to learn 64 combinations of raised dots for letters, numbers, and small phrases.

She grasped them quickly, confirming Bell's assertion that it was not her disabilities that were holding her back, but a lack of opportunity and training.

As her language skills improved, Helen applied to and was accepted by Radcliffe College, becoming the first deaf-blind person enrolled in university anywhere.

With Anne at her side, working as diligently as ever, Helen became the first deaf-blind person to receive an undergraduate degree.

After graduation, Helen turned her efforts toward activism. She knew that she was one of the lucky ones because she had been given Anne. Many others in her situation were not so fortunate.

Her motivation for activism came in part from her concern about blindness and other disabilities, and society's seeming indifference to their cause. As she wrote:

> I was appointed on a commission to investigate the conditions of the blind. For the first time I, who had thought blindness a misfortune beyond human control, found that too much of it was traceable to wrong industrial conditions, often caused by the selfishness and greed of employers. And the social evil contributed its share. I found that poverty drove women to a life of shame that ended in blindness.

In 1920 Helen became one of the founders of the American Civil Liberties Union. In that same decade she sent a donation to the National Association for the Advancement of Colored People, with letters of support that appeared in their magazine *The Crisis*.

She who had so little herself, who had been cruelly cut off from the world as a baby, became a beacon of hope and a voice for the blind and deaf around the world.

She did fundraising tours for the American Foundation for the Blind, and fought to advance the living and working conditions of blind people, many of whom were poorly educated and living in asylums. Her efforts played a major part in improving these conditions and in helping change the way society viewed the blind and deaf.

Then tragedy struck again.

In 1936, following numerous illnesses, Helen's lifelong mentor and companion Anne Sullivan died. While it was a staggering loss to Helen, she knew that Anne would have wanted her to continue their work. And so she did, astoundingly, for another 30 years.

After World War II, Helen and her secretary circled the globe fundraising for the American Foundation for the Overseas Blind.

She was always the voice, always the beacon, never tiring of standing up for people like her. These were people who had been robbed of the gift of sight and hearing and were expected to function in a society that neither understood them nor, for the most part, gave a damn about them.

In her last years, Helen was awarded the Presidential Medal of Freedom, the nation's highest civilian award. A year later, at the 1939 New York World's Fair, she was voted into the Women's Hall of Fame.

On June 1, 1968, after 88 years of struggle, Helen died silently and peacefully in her sleep.

What is the mark that Helen Keller leaves us after a life spent bettering the world for people with sensory disabilities?

I think it is simply this. Helen and Anne showed us that our value as human beings is not how well we function physically or even mentally. Disability does not mean inability.

Helen Keller's mark was showing us that greatness is determined by how much we give, not how much we get.

Ponderables

Count your blessings.

That is the first thing Helen Keller's story constantly prompts me to remember.

Have you ever spent just a few minutes to count the things in life you are lucky to have? It is a wonderful thing to do, especially on those bad days when nothing is going right. Perspective has a way of changing things quickly.

How do you judge people's abilities – by how they appear on the outside, or by their character, their effort, or their results? Most of us judge by what we see on the outside, and by that measure Helen Keller would have ended up in an institution.

How patient are you? Would you have had the patience of Anne Sullivan to start from nothing to try to teach someone to communicate?

I wish that kind of patience on every parent alive.

Team Hoyt

All you need is love.
– Lennon and McCartney

Most of us have someone or something in our lives of which we say, "We are not worthy."

There are many such stories in **The Mark of a Leader**, but for me, this one may be the most powerful.

It is the story of a man who many people feel is the world's greatest dad. It is the story of his son, who is a champion in every sense of the word. It is the story of them together, as a team.

It is the story of 1+1=11.

And it is one of my all-time favorite stories proving that you can do anything if you make up your mind to do it.

Read it and be inspired to do that thing, right now, that you think is impossible.

In 1967, John Lennon and Paul McCartney put forth a simple philosophy that all we really need is love to get us through the adversities of life.

Was this the naïve songwriting of two young idealists, or a deeper insight into the human condition?

Cynics would claim it was the former. Dick and Rick Hoyt would not.

In 1962, Dick and his wife, Judy, gave birth to their first child, Rick. Baby Rick got tangled in his umbilical cord on the way to this earth and was born a spastic quadriplegic with cerebral palsy – unable to move or talk.

But it was clear to his parents that he could hear, and that he knew exactly what was going on around him.

Their pastor put their options simply: either put him in an institution and forget about him, or try to give him as close to a normal life as you can – loving and nurturing him and taking it one day at a time.

They chose the latter. They did their best to give Rick a normal life, beginning a lifelong battle against society to integrate him into the mainstream.

It was not easy. Sadly, most of us do not know how to deal with others who are not "normal."

But Rick persevered, with the help of his parents and two brothers.

One day, while still a high school student, Rick was watching a local college basketball game and saw a sign promoting a weekend race. The sign said:

RUN FOR DOOGIE

Those three words would change his life.

A student by that name had just been in an automobile accident and was left paralyzed. The school had organized a five-mile charity race to raise funds to help pay his medical bills.

Rick obviously could relate to Doogie's crisis, and he went home that night and asked his dad if they could go in the race together. Dick said yes.

So there they were: Dick, a military man, not an athlete, and his son, Rick, virtually unable to move. The plan, if there was one, was that Dick would simply push Rick in his wheelchair, which at the time had wheels like a shopping cart.

Most people expected them to go to the first corner and turn around. They underestimated Team Hoyt.

Dick could barely walk when they finished – the pain and the blisters on his feet and hands were unbelievable. But finish they did, second to last.

That night on the computer that had been made to allow him to type out messages, Rick wrote, "Dad, when we're running I feel like I don't have a disability."

With that one sentence Rick, who could not move unaided, changed the Hoyts' lives and those of people around the world.

Rick and Dick started competing in races with the help of their family. Over the next several years they ran together every weekend, loving this new-found passion together.

Because they lived in the Boston area, it was only a matter of time before they set their sights on the biggie – the Boston Marathon.

They were not allowed to participate officially, because they didn't fit the categories. They would get in the way of the serious runners, and couldn't run with the wheelchairs because Dick was pushing. Amazingly, many of the other contestants, including the handicapped, were among those blocking their entrance to the race.

So they entered unofficially. It took three years of entering and competing – never finishing last and each time finishing nearer the middle of the pack – until they were allowed to enter officially.

The sight of Dick pushing his son to complete a marathon

caused jaws to drop, hearts to melt, and cheers to erupt along the racecourse.

This was not simply about running, about testing your personal endurance. This was an act of love between a father and son. And no one who saw it could be the same again.

Suddenly the Hoyts were a draw. They were invited to race after race, and then, one day, they were invited to compete in a triathlon.

The first one, in Western Canada, was no big deal: 1 mile of swimming, 40 miles of biking, and 4 miles of running. Heck, most of us do that before breakfast on Saturday, right?

Of course they said yes.

Now, there were a few challenges. Running they had done. But Dick was in his 40s and did not really know how to swim. And how exactly would he get Rick through 40 miles of bicycling?

Never one to be slowed down by anything, Dick learned to swim. With the help of some military buddies, he rigged up a raft and harness to pull Rick through the water, and a front carriage seat for a bike.

They practiced together. When Rick wasn't there, Dick practiced by pulling and pushing a 100-lb bag of sand.

Once again, fans were worried about whether the Hoyts could make it. The worry was unfounded. They competed and finished the triathlon – again, near the back but not last.

They were hooked. They continued to do marathons and triathlons until one day they took on the ultimate challenge: Ironman Hawaii.

Try this next Saturday: 2.4 miles of Pacific Ocean swimming, 112 miles of biking, and then a simple 26-mile marathon to finish it off.

Race organizers were worried about their safety, but by then everyone who knew the Hoyts knew that when Dick and Rick made up their minds, they would not be stopped.

The first year, they failed. They ran into problems in the Pacific Ocean and could not continue.

It was demoralizing, but just a minor setback. And to Ironman's eternal credit, they encouraged the pair to return the following year. Return they did, finishing the race and contributing another chapter to the world's athletic folklore.

By now they were world celebrities. They established the Hoyt Fund to raise awareness for handicapped people and encourage their integration into mainstream society.

In 1992, they got even more ambitious, if that is possible. They ran across the United States – from Los Angeles to Boston. Forty-three days on the road. Across mountains. Across desert. Across it all. Raising awareness for the handicapped and raising money for their fund.

From there, the invitations started to come in from around the world. They began speaking at corporate events and fundraisers. Network television focused their cameras on them. The Hoyts were a story that no one could ever forget.

In the more than 25 years since they ran their first race, Rick and Dick have been in well over 900 competitions – mostly marathons and triathlons. That is a pace of 36 per year, more than any healthy single athlete on earth typically does.

They continue to compete to this day, despite the fact that Dick, now retired, had a heart attack a few years ago. Doctors said it would have felled a man in lesser physical condition.

And Rick? Well, he lives an amazing life. He is happy. He is very competitive. He has graduated from high school and college. He lives today in an apartment on his own, aided by care workers. He has a job designing programs for the disabled at a local college. He and Dick are on the speaking circuit, both raising money for their fund and encouraging people with disabilities of all kinds.

And, of course, they continue to participate in marathons or triathlons whenever they can.

Now, the story of Team Hoyt is astounding and inspiring by any measure. Their message to the world is that you can do anything if you make up your mind to do it. And, without question, they have shown that to be true. That is their mark.

But here is an interesting question: If athletes require both a strong mind and a strong body to be successful, who is the athlete here? Dick, who does the physical work – who runs, swims, and bikes? Or Rick, who provides the emotional fuel and the drive to do it?

Dick is the first to say that he could not and would not do this without Rick. Rick challenges him. He keeps him going when others fall. And Rick, of course, could not do this without Dick.

If you look at all great human accomplishment, you will be hard pressed to find something great that was done by an individual. Time and time again we have been shown that if you want to do something great, you have to have a great team. That truth lies at the very heart of the human condition. Nothing great was ever done alone. And you will be hard pressed to find a more poignant example than Team Hoyt.

There is another mark that Dick and Rick Hoyt leave for us all as well: Be careful how you judge others.

We all know that. But we sometimes forget it in practice. Just remember, the man sitting beside you in that wheelchair – the one with no control of his body, who can barely move and who cannot talk – that man may just be half of one of the greatest competitive sporting teams in history. He may have completed a triathlon last weekend.

How about you?

Oh, and by the way, I think Lennon and McCartney were right. Love may not be **all** we need, but damn, it sure helps.

You can find out more about Team Hoyt on their website:
www.teamhoyt.com.

Buy their book. Buy their DVD. Bring them to your next conference.
Give to their charity if you can.
You will be amazed.

Ponderables

I love the saying, *"Impossible is a state of mind."* Rick and Dick Hoyt certainly prove it to me.

Is there anything in your life that you always felt was impossible to achieve?

Is it really impossible, or have you just never spent the time and effort to figure out how to achieve it?

What would you do if you knew you could not fail?

Jackie Robinson

Life is not a spectator sport. If you're going to spend your whole life in the grandstand just watching what goes on, in my opinion you're wasting your life.
– Jackie Robinson

As I write this book, fear has changed the face of the world once again. The attacks of 9/11, the ongoing turmoil in the Middle East, religious fanaticism, crackpots freely buying guns, oil shortages, global warming, and the proliferation of nukes have all created a climate of fear across much of the world.

Most of us, though, are not personally touched by these fears every day. We are inconvenienced at the airport. We pay more for a tank of gas. We don't let our kids go out alone. That's about it.

But that doesn't mean we're not afraid.

What we are afraid of, and what we choose to do about it, has a huge effect on our lives.

For some of us, fears are debilitating. They hold us back, lock us into our comfort zones, prevent us from taking chances.

For others, fear is a great motivator.

The fear of failure is often cited as one of the most powerful drivers of successful people.

But fear of failure is a rational fear.

To me the most dangerous fears are those that spring from hatred. Because hatred is not logical. And deep hatred seemingly knows no bounds. If someone hates you badly enough, you have a good reason to be afraid, to run and hide.

This is the story of a man who refused to do so, and who helped change the face of sport as a result.

How tough is your job?

What kinds of distractions do you deal with when you're trying to work?

How are you treated by your co-workers, customers, and competitors?

Do you wake up and jump out of bed excited about working another day?

Or do you wonder if you'll make it through to dinner?

Here's some perspective for you.

You're a young boy in America in the 1930s. Born in the south to a poor family. Your dad just disappears one day.

Like so many other kids, you love sports. And you're pretty good at them. Good enough that you could probably get a scholarship if you worked at it. So you do. You work at what you love to play, guided by a loving single mother.

Ultimately, you choose UCLA, where you become the first student ever to letter in four sports.

You narrow your choice down to baseball. You can hit like a cannon, you can run like a gazelle, and you can catch anything. You can even pitch a little. You're definitely good enough to turn pro.

There's just one problem. For you, turning pro isn't the Major Leagues, it's a different league altogether: the Negro Leagues. Because, you see, you're guilty of being black in America. And in the 1930s and '40s, blacks didn't play professional baseball in the Major Leagues. It just wasn't done.

Jackie Robinson believed the American dream that he was taught as a kid. All men are born equal. One nation under God. The value of freedom, for which his forefathers had fought so hard.

He knew this wasn't true when he was a kid, because there

were different rules for black kids and white kids – way different rules.

But participation in sports, he thought, was decided by skill, not by color. If you were good enough, you got to play, right?

Well, not really. See, there was this thing called fear. Not his fear. A lot of white folks' fear. Unfortunately it came around wearing the mask of hate, looking for someone like him. Someone colored.

In 1945, Jackie Robinson joined the Kansas City Monarchs of the American Negro League. He was so good that Branch Rickey, GM of the Brooklyn Dodgers, signed him to play the following season for the Montreal Royals – the Dodgers' top Minor League team. He was paid a $3,500 bonus, plus $600 per month.

Rickey was reviled for his gamble, but it paid off. Robinson led the Royals to the "Little World Series" title, scoring the winning run in the seventh game.

The following season, he became the first black player to get called up to baseball's Major Leagues. This was a white man's game, and even his teammates on the Brooklyn Dodgers didn't understand why a "colored" could make it onto their team.

Didn't much matter that he was better than all of them. He was going to have to share a shower and a bus with them.

Now that just ain't right, is it?

What are your distractions at work again?

Jackie Robinson and his family received death threats most days. The threats were particularly vile on game days, when callers would describe the horrors that would happen to his wife and kids while he was at the ballpark.

Oh, he was in their sights too – literally. Some callers said they'd be sitting in the bleachers with a gun, just waiting for their chance to get him.

All the while, young Jackie was expected to keep his eye on the ball and help win the game.

Baseball is a game of inches. It has been argued that the most difficult action in sports is hitting a ball thrown from 60 feet 6 inches away, off a raised mound, at speeds over 90 miles an hour. It's hard enough to do when the pitcher puts the ball in, or at least near, the strike zone. But when Robinson went to the plate, the opposing pitchers liked to throw the ball at his head at 90 miles an hour, while the fans booed, taunted, and threw garbage at him.

Most of us would have gone home and taken up some other game – like croquet.

But Jackie Robinson knew that someone had to break the barrier. Someone had to take a stand and put up with the humiliation and, more important, the fear. Perhaps he understood that, despite the threats, it would be hard to kill a Major League baseball player and get away with it. And maybe that understanding gave him the power to continue.

He could not argue. Hatred knows no logic. His only chance was to play baseball so well that his critics and the fans would be silenced. However grudgingly, they would be forced to have respect.

So that's what he did. He played his heart out. In his first season with the Brooklyn Dodgers he was the National League's Rookie of the Year.

And here is a sample of what else he accomplished despite the threats, the beanballs, and the garbage:

- MVP in 1949, batting .342
- Six National League pennants in 10 seasons
- One World Series
- The first black player inducted into the Baseball Hall of Fame

He retired from baseball in 1957 after a glorious ten-year career that changed the sport for every non-white who has played the game since. His achievement, along with those of pioneers like the Harlem Globetrotters, helped open the door, albeit at different speeds, for every other sport in America as well.

Jackie Robinson's courage changed a society. He became an icon of hope to African-American parents and their kids across America.

Perhaps as important as his courage was his character. This was an athlete from the old school. A polite, gracious, humble man who knew he was lucky to be able to do what he loved in his life and who served as a role model for kids and adults everywhere.

Jackie Robinson took the high ground. Always. And in doing so set an example that could not be denied.

Asked his opinion of his detractors, he replied, *"I'm not concerned with your liking or disliking me. All I ask is that you respect me as a human being."*

Respect him they did. Because even the white trash racists and hatemongers could not deny that, in sport, the numbers tell the truth.

Jackie went on to a successful business career and tireless work on behalf of the NAACP. Since its inception, his foundation has given away thousands of scholarships to needy and deserving kids.

But in addition to opening the door for so many, Jackie Robinson left a deeper mark. He showed us all that hatred is born from fear. And fear only has power if we give it power.

Jackie Robinson looked fear and hatred in the eye and refused to blink. And he helped change a society as a result.

Ponderables

We are all afraid. Sometimes our fear drives us on to better performance. But often it holds us back, keeping us in our comfort zones.

Have you ever identified the things you are afraid of? It is a useful exercise, because once you identify at least your major fears, you can begin to understand and overcome them if they are holding you back.

If you could live your life totally fearlessly – if you could just "give up" fear – what things would you do that you are not doing?

So what's holding you back?

Muhammad Ali

You want me to be great,
but you don't ever want me to say, "I'm great"?
– Kanye West

We live in a society that loves to create celebrities and then knock them down. We put the beautiful, the talented, or just the well-promoted on pedestals. We tell them how wonderful they are. We stalk them with cameras. We violate their privacy and declare our intrusion the price of fame. We inspect their every move.

And then we smile and buy the magazines when they cannot possibly live up to the exaggerated expectations we have created for them.

On their way up, we expect humility from those who are great. We adore them because they are the best – because they are better than we are. But we don't want them to say so. We want them to be "aw shucks" humble, even though we and millions of others and our wallets are telling them how wonderful they are.

So there is a paradox for those who aspire to greatness. You have to believe you are the greatest, but you will get shot down if you say you are.

I guess that's ultimately the price of fame.

What is greatness to you?

The most wins?

The most money?

The CEO's job?

The most awards?

The most people calling you their friend?

The most people helped by you when they need it?

The most people at your funeral?

In sports, greatness is measured by numbers – performance. Wins, points, medals. The more you get, the greater you are. In most sports, you can get to at least a short list of the greatest by the numbers. After that it is usually subjective.

Now, to be the best at something, you have to believe that you can be and that you are the best. It is not possible to be the best without believing that you are.

Cassius Marcellus Clay understood this paradox deeply. He knew that to be the best, he had to believe that he was the best. And he knew he had to say it, because our words create our reality.

What we say is what we think. What we think is what we are.

So, perhaps unlike any sportsman who had come before, Ali set out to become the greatest, in part by declaring, *"I am the greatest."*

Many perceived his bravado as arrogance, a lack of respect for those who came before him, and a general contempt for his peers and contemporaries. In reality, the contrary was the case. This was a man who was ahead of Anthony Robbins' time.

Clay would explain that as a young man, he quickly learned the value of self-aggrandizement and flamboyance. They were tools in the toolkit along with the punches, the dancing, the bobbing and weaving.

He used his obvious good looks and charisma as a promotional tool. He used boasting and audacious statements to raise attendance levels and purses. It was another way to be the one everyone wanted to see. And he had the talent to back his mouth up.

He used his self-confidence to try to bring doubt into the minds of his opponents. "If he is that sure of himself," they might wonder, "could it be that maybe, just maybe, he's right?" Sport is a game of inches and nanoseconds. That one thought alone could open up a hole big enough to land a knockout punch.

Cassius Clay burst onto the fight scene like a bomb – young, brash, good-looking, and loud – and started to win big. He won at the Olympics and returned home ready to become the greatest.

At first, of course, America didn't take too kindly to this brash young man from Louisville. Who was this uppity Negro anyway?

He was a young man who won virtually every fight he was given, that's who.

As if his mouth wasn't enough, he abandoned what he called his "slave name," converted to Islam, and changed his name to Muhammad Ali. It was not a snap decision – Ali was a deeply religious man.

"I don't have to be what you want me to be; I'm free to be what I want," he proclaimed in announcing his rejection of the American dream, a value system he found wanting.

The recording artist Prince changes his name every few years and no one notices. But in the 1960s, it was a different world. Shunning the American dream – well, it was just not done! A lot of people quietly hoped that someone would give Ali a good whupping and shut him up.

But that wasn't so easy to do. In boxing, you can't beat 'em if you can't hit 'em. He worked his way through the boxing ranks, scoring victory after victory. And then he used his mouth to challenge the heavyweight champion Sonny Liston to a fight.

Liston refused, which only got the mouth going louder and faster. Ali called him a chicken. That got the attention of the media. In a sport where the champions were neither too pretty nor too talkative, he was just what a sportswriter needed – a handsome, smart, mouthy boxer who could win.

Eventually Liston had no choice but to fight him. The run-up to the fight created incredible excitement. Most people didn't give Ali a chance and secretly hoped Liston would shut him up for good.

But Ali delivered what his words had promised and destroyed Liston to become the boxing heavyweight champion of the world.

Of course, the new champ was not what others wanted him to be.

He became even more devoutly Muslim, in a predominantly Judeo-Christian society. Then, in 1967, he refused to join the army to serve in Vietnam, citing religious grounds and saying, *"I ain't got no quarrel with them Vietcong ... No Vietcong never called me nigger!"*

Once he had declared himself, public opinion was instantaneous, passionate, and disapproving. Many reporters and boxing officials refused to recognize his new name, and some went so far as to demand that his title be revoked.

Sadly, they were heard.

Ali stood by his convictions during the ongoing backlash,

refusing to bow to public demands to go back on his deeply felt religious convictions.

The American media, with the exception of famed sportscaster Howard Cosell, vilified him for his unpatriotic stance and lack of sympathy for the war. The government prosecuted him as a draft dodger and revoked his passport. To their eternal shame, the National Boxing Commission and virtually every state bowed to the pressure and pulled his license, leaving him unable to fight for three and a half years at the peak of his professional career.

Unable to earn a living, and having lost the initial court battle, he faced a five-year prison term. But he would not succumb.

That was the power of his belief in himself and his values.

During his exile from the sport he loved, he supported himself through speaking engagements, using his status as a former world champion to continue speaking out against the oppression of blacks and against America's involvement in Vietnam.

Ali became a broadly idolized symbol of black pride and resistance because of his unshakable aversion to yielding to the authorities.

In June 1970, the U.S. Supreme Court reversed his conviction and supported his claim as a conscientious objector. Ali was free of the looming possibility of jail time and recovered his passport, free to travel and fight wherever he chose.

His triumphant return to boxing was amazing. In true form for a man of his character, instead of suing for his title reinstatement, he recovered the title the same way he had won it previously: in the ring.

In 1974, in perhaps the greatest fight ever, dubbed "The Rumble in the Jungle," Ali came back against champion George Foreman. The fight was held in Zaire. Two African Americans squaring off in the jungle.

As always, Ali was brash and verbal. The publicity was enormous. And in a strange way, the fight became social: he, the people's champion, against Foreman, representing the establishment.

Ali destroyed Foreman, as he said he would, in the eighth round.

By now, Muhammad Ali was as much about social justice and anti-racism as he was about boxing.

He said, *"I wanted to establish a relationship between American blacks and Africans."*

While in Africa, Ali changed. He would meet with the people, speak to them, and hear their stories – stories about his roots. And in so doing he added another trait to his dynamic personality: compassion.

He had matured, not just as a fighter, but as a man. He became a champion on a whole new level. He became a champion of human rights.

He continued boxing for another seven years, until he retired in 1981.

His record: three times World Heavyweight Champion and a record of 51-5.

In 1984 it was announced that the man named "the greatest athlete of all time" was suffering from Parkinson's disease, a condition that cruelly limits his motor skills and inhibits his once extensive public speaking.

For a man who plied his physical prowess all of his life, and who used his quick mental and verbal skills as weapons, to be so cruelly brought to his knees must have been excruciating.

But in classic Ali form, he has not let his illness stop him from being free to do as he feels. And his struggle with Parkinson's has only elevated his status as a mythological hero.

Whether he goes down in history as the greatest boxer of all time is surely not something he cares about any more. More significant to all of us is that he lived his life and career on his terms – proud, defiant, and with bravado, a hero that anyone could look up to.

Ultimately I think the mark of Muhammad Ali will be this simple lesson he put forth for us all: If you want to be great, you have to stand up and speak up for what you believe in. It may not always be popular. Sometimes it will be dangerous. But if you don't stand up for the things you believe in, no one else will.

Ponderables

Have you ever written down your values?
What are your top three?

How far would you go to defend or support your
values?

How do you keep them front and center
every day?

What do you want to be known for, whatever it is
that you do? Your business or artistic success? Your
kids? Your giving?

If you could have met Muhammad Ali in the prime
of his career, perhaps casually over dinner, what one
question would you have asked him?

What one thing would you tell him you stand for?

Terry Fox

*I just wish people would realize that anything
is possible if you try.
Dreams are made if people try.*
– Terry Fox

Terry Fox is one of my greatest heroes. It would
be easy to argue that he was the greatest and most
courageous Canadian of the 20th century.

His impact was so profound that you need merely
mention his name to most grown Canadians and you
will see a tear well up in their eye, as it is right now in
mine as I type.

For those of you who do not know him, he was a
young man struck at age 19 by cancer. He lost one
leg above the knee. During his stay in hospital he
witnessed firsthand the tragedy that cancer wreaks
on human life at all ages. He knew the only hope was
research to find a cure. So he decided to run across
Canada on his one remaining leg to raise money for
cancer research.

He called his run the Marathon of Hope.

He didn't really run or walk. He had a kind of hop,
and you could tell that every step he took was
incredibly painful.

That hop inspired millions of people and continues to do so to this day.

It is 4:30 in the morning. You can feel the cold predawn air on your face, but you are not cold. In fact, your body is hot.

You are on the side of a road. Alone with your thoughts, your breathing, and your footsteps.

Occasionally a truck will challenge your right to the road, sometimes blaring its horn. Or a dog might take offense at your breaking the silence of the morning and warn you off with its bark.

But when they have quieted, you are once again left with only the small team that accompanies you.

You are running. For life, but not your life.

You have been running at a pace that has never been attempted before in known history, and will likely never be duplicated. It is a pace that most people said was impossible.

But then, you aren't most people.

For over 140 days, you have run a marathon every day. At least 26 miles, with almost no days off.

Typically, marathon runners will complete a race and then take a break for a few days or a week before even considering running another race. Their bodies need that time to recuperate.

So does yours. But you don't have time to rest – every minute is too precious to you. So you gulp down water to stave off the dehydration and you eat oranges to give you energy. And you keep going.

Like all marathoners, you fight against constant pain. There is a pain in your chest, but it usually goes away after some running.

Your legs, though – that's a different story. Chafing, blisters, even cysts. The ache from the constant battering never stops. It is a pain that most people cannot begin to comprehend.

Yet you never complain. Ever.

Your marathon pace is astounding on its own. But at the beginning and end of most days, without a rest, you have other critical obligations. You meet with people. Ordinary people, townsfolk from wherever you are that day, and most important, the media. For they tell your story.

You talk in honest, ordinary language. People of all ages listen in awe.

No one who sees you is ever the same again. They cannot be. Your courage is so inspiring, your mission so full of hope, that they are elevated to a place they have never been.

Often they cry, but the tears are not the simple tears of sorrow. These tears are born in the greatness of your spirit, for that is what you share with them: the irrepressible grandeur of the human spirit. It burns in you like a flame. And it will never go out. They will make sure of that, even if you cannot.

You will collapse in your small bed tonight, get up before the sun tomorrow, put on a pair of worn gray shorts, a dirty T-shirt, and a beat-up old pair of blue sneakers, and run another marathon.

Some days the sun will scorch your face. Other days, the rain or sleet will burn you. You will stagger up the steep hills and stumble down the other side. Dogs will attack you. The wind will blow gently on your back and too often hard upon your face.

And still you will run.

As your race unfolds, you will increasingly be followed by police and by people of all ages and backgrounds. They will come out to touch your spirit. To give, to run beside you, and to cheer you on.

And then one day, the pain in your chest will not relent. Your body will give in. You will be forced to stop running.

This part of your marathon will end.

While you are not able to complete your journey, your dream

will not die. Far from it. Because your dream, and your courage, have lifted the spirit of millions of people. You have touched their souls and left an indelible mark.

When you finally succumb to your disease, you will be mourned by more people than for the world's greatest celebrities or politicians. And your mourners will represent all walks of life and every conceivable age group. You have become a hero for the people, and they will never forget you.

Today, over 25 years later, your story continues to be told. And as it is told, hundreds of millions of dollars are given so that one day others will not suffer the way you did.

In fact, the irony of your story is that, thanks to the research money you have raised, today you probably would have been able to complete your marathon.

Instead, others run in your place every year. Hundreds of thousands of them, in countries right around the world. People who never saw you but who were stirred by your quest, just as you had wished.

All running in memory of you – a 22-year-old kid who was dealt a staggering blow, and made a courageous decision about how to respond.

You taught us well, and you will not be forgotten.

For your name is Terry Fox. And you are a leader in the most profound sense of the word.

And what is your mark, Terry Fox?
I think it is this.

Each of us has our own marathon to run. Our own life. Along our own road. We may choose that road, but we never know how far we will get along it. All we know is that we must move forward and do it one step at a time.

Terry Fox, you taught us to put everything we have into every single step along the way.

You can support Terry Fox's fight against cancer by participating in a Terry Fox run near you, or by donating through his foundation to fund cancer research.

*You can find out more about him and his amazing story and donate to his cause at **www.terryfoxrun.org.***

*There is also an incredible book about him entitled **Terry**, by Douglas Coupland. It is one of the most powerful books you will ever enjoy. Read, and you will never forget it.*

Ponderables

Terry Fox, to me, is more than a role model. He is a hero.

Who are your heroes?

What have they influenced you to do?

Have you shared their stories with your kids if you have them?

What do you do to keep the stories of heroes alive in your family and circle of friends?

The Visionaries

Dame Anita Roddick
& The Body Shop

If you think you are too small to have an impact,
try going to bed with a mosquito.
– Anita Roddick

Every company has – or should have – some form of vision, mission, and values statement. This statement describes the direction, purpose, and principles on which the company is built. It is designed to be a compass for employees, customers, investors, the media, and the financial community.

Most vision and values statements are well-intended but hollow lists that cater neither to the human imagination nor to the human spirit. They are designed by committee and, with all the care given a legal document, sanitized for accuracy and political correctness.

I have worked with hundreds of companies. Very seldom have I seen a vision or mission that made me say, "Wow! I want to be part of that." Very seldom have I found employees who can recite or even capture the main points of their organization's statement.

If someone has to **read** you their purpose, then the

point has definitely been missed.

Not all businesses are "wow." Some sad businesses think "wow" is unnecessary – fluff. But I think of "wow" as the right-brained part of any organization – the imaginative and emotional side.

Without these, companies are just jobs. They may make money, but typically they are just employment factories, often characterized by high turnover.

To create "wow" – something that captures the imagination and emotions of their people, their customers, and their stakeholders – more and more companies are tying the purpose of their organization to the communities they serve. They are reaching for a higher value than just making money for investors.

This is often called social responsibility, and it is not just the right thing to do, it is good business.

In the words of Anita Roddick: *"Political awareness and activism must be woven into the fabric of business – to do otherwise is to be not merely an ostrich, but criminally irresponsible."*

Starbucks was built with higher values from the ground up. Interface retooled their entire business, at incredible cost, in order to be environmentally responsible. A bank in my community "owns" a huge annual walk for breast cancer research. That alone is enough to differentiate them within the commodity business of banking. And there are many, many others.

Here's a story of one of the first big-brand companies to successfully tie their mission to the world they served. The company defined and separated the brand. The brand drove their behavior. And it ignited their success because it gave people a reason to buy their products.

Every business today can learn from this pioneer.

Ecological responsibility. That's not what most retailers would say their business stands for.

Yet it was from that simple vision that Dame Anita Roddick started and grew the global Body Shop retail chain, arguably one of the most important businesses of the 20th century.

Anita was born to an Italian immigrant family in Britain. Her mother ran a café and taught her daughter the importance of recycling to save money.

As an intelligent, adventurous, and independent young

woman, Anita traveled extensively and got a very different view of the world than most of her peers at home. One of the things that stood out in that view was how people around the world used natural products to care for their bodies. And how recycling and reusing were part of their way of life.

As she wrote:

> When you have lived six months with a group that has been rubbing their bodies with cocoa butter, and those bodies are magnificent, or you wash your hair with mud and it works, you go on to break all sorts of conventions, from personal ethics to body care. Then, if you're like me, you develop this stunning love for anthropology.

In 1970, Anita ceased her roaming ways and married Gordon Roddick. Over the next few years they opened a restaurant and a hotel and had two children. But the business wore them down, and, having no time to spend with each other and their kids, they decided to sell.

Gordon set off on an adventure in the Americas. Anita needed to fund his absence while caring for two small children. So in 1976 she opened a natural cosmetics store in a small space beside a funeral home in nearby Brighton.

The shop sold a small line of handmade products, packaged in urine sample bottles because she could not afford anything better. Anita explained her practice as follows:

It wasn't only economic necessity that inspired the birth of The Body Shop. My early travels had given me a wealth of experience. I had spent time in farming and fishing communities with pre-industrial peoples, and been exposed to body rituals of women from all over the world. Also the frugality that my mother exercised during the war years made me question retail conventions. Why waste a container when you can refill it? And why buy more of something than you can use?

We behaved as she did in the Second World War, we reused everything, we refilled everything and we recycled all we could. The foundation of The Body Shop's environmental activism was born out of ideas like these.

It is sad how many of us have forgotten the lessons of our parents and grandparents, learned as recently as World War II.

This simple, frugal approach prompted Anita to ask customers to bring the bottles back for refilling. That created repeat customers.

Her small line of products was inspired by those used by indigenous people whom she had seen in her years of travel. Unlike most "beauty" shops, she made no promises of erasing years off a woman's face.

Instead, Anita offered *"a two-for-one sale no other cosmetic company could ever hope to match: buy a bottle of 'natural' lotion and get social justice for free."*

Recycling bottles. A cosmetics shop that made no ridiculous promises. And, as it turns out, green walls.

Put those together with good timing, and you have the birth of a brand. *"I am aware that success is more than a good idea,"* writes Anita. *"It is timing, too. The Body Shop arrived just as Europe was going 'green.' The Body Shop has always been recognizable by its green color, the only color that we could find to cover the damp, moldy walls of my first shop."*

Recycling became Anita's way of business, and she realized more and more that her customers shared her values about the world and the environment.

The Body Shop was a magnet for them. Young idealists and aging hippies alike suddenly found a business that stood for something other than just profit, and they became loyal customers.

Anita defined the premise of the business as *"Profit with Principle."*

She opened a second shop within six months, getting some financing from a neighbor (one of the greatest investments of all time). Gordon returned to England and came up with the idea of self-financed stores – franchising. Body Shops began to pop up everywhere.

At the same time, the chain's commitment to their core principles became more clearly defined. Anita hated the cosmetics industry. As she says, *"It's lies, deceits, and false promises,"* particularly to women. The Body Shop honed its raison d'être with a mission statement that includes these words:

> To dedicate our business to the pursuit of social and
> environmental change. To creatively balance the
> financial and human needs of our stakeholders:
> employees, customers, franchisees, suppliers, and
> shareholders. To courageously ensure that our
> business is ecologically sustainable, meeting the
> needs of the present without compromising the
> future. To meaningfully contribute to local, national,
> and international communities in which we trade,
> by adopting a code of conduct which ensures care,
> honesty, fairness, and respect.

Pare that down so you can remember it and you get:

1) Be committed to social and environmental change
2) Be financially responsible to stakeholders
3) Be ecologically sustainable
4) Contribute to our communities
5) Treat people as we would like to be treated

I can remember those ideas.

Apparently I am not alone. By 1982, new shops were opening
at a rate of two per month. Roddick's refusal to test products
on animals got massive PR for The Body Shop. There were 2,500
applications for franchises in the United States alone.

Some would argue that the tipping point, good or bad, came in
1985 when they took the company public. Roddick was
outspokenly critical of the business world for its emphasis on

wealth over job creation, and denounced as shallow and unimportant the beauty and cosmetics industry that was making her rich.

There are rules for public companies. They typically don't take a stand, because that involves risk. The Body Shop took a stand on everything, supported Greenpeace, fought against unfair trade practices in Third World countries, and all the while tried to make a profit for the shareholders.

In 1990 The Body Shop Foundation was established, a charity that funds human rights and environmental protection groups. This was but one of many formal initiatives that helped the chain make a difference in the community on issues ranging from the environment to the homeless to Fair Trade practices to animal rights.

Of course, every success comes with criticism. By the mid-1990s, Roddick's critics were starting to be heard.

She was savaged her for alleged hypocrisy – people charged that her principles-before-profits stance was just a marketing ploy. But Roddick fought back, and almost all of the charges proved untrue.

Today, The Body Shop has over 2,100 stores in 55 markets serving over 75 million customers. It has been globally recognized with awards for virtually all of its policies on fair trade, community support, animal testing, environmental responsibility, and ethics. In short, it has been honored for the principles – the vision – that Anita instilled into the very foundation of the company from the day it began.

Anita and her husband, Gordon, long ago moved on to a life of social and political activism, having given away a huge part of their money. They are global leaders of the "vigilante consumerism" movement, encouraging anyone who will listen to force businesses to be socially and environmentally responsible.

The Body Shop was bought out in 2006 by L'Oreal and runs as a separate entity in the L'Oreal family of companies. Whether this will be good or bad for the future of the company remains to be seen.

Anita Roddick's mark, meanwhile, is still evolving.

Without doubt she was one of the most important business people of the 20th century. She single-handedly changed the face of 20th-century retailing and set a benchmark for entrepreneurs and women in business everywhere to create great companies that make a difference.

She also began the first global, high-profile company whose social values were tightly woven into the very way it did business. They were not the first to do this, but they were the most significant in bringing it to the public's attention.

Today, social responsibility – the principles by which a corporation runs its business in relation to the environment and the communities it serves – is one of the hottest issues facing CEOs. And increasingly their positions are being directly reflected in the value of their companies.

Companies that are responsible corporate citizens, that are truly committed to the world in which they operate, are being rewarded with loyalty, passion, energy, and great bottom line results.

Much of the thanks for this must be placed at the feet of Dame Anita.

But it is our belief that her biggest impact has yet to be truly felt.

With the emergence of China and India, the global market is about to be transformed. These two huge markets are quickly evolving from relatively undeveloped to wealthy economies. Already, millions of factory workers in the Americas and Europe have been left unemployed as their owners have moved factories to China to reduce labor costs. Barely subsisting on minimal wages already, these workers face a future that is bleak at best.

When price is more important than social conscience, the casualties are usually human.

So Anita's biggest battle has probably just begun. Based on her track record, only a fool would bet against her having a major influence on the future of global consumerism.

Let's hope I'm right.

> You can find out what Anita Roddick is doing today and get involved at **www.anitaroddick.com.**

Ponderables

I believe that one of the most important issues facing CEOs in the next few decades will be their platform of social responsibility. It will drive investment decisions, CEO paychecks, and customer loyalty.

The Body Shop was a big influence on me as an entrepreneur because it showed me that you can make money while making a difference. Its founders didn't set out to make a difference because they thought it would help the bottom line. They did it because it was the right thing to do.

Here are a few questions that Anita Roddick has prompted me to ask:

What does my company stand for? What is our vision – where do we want to be? What is our mission – what will we do to get there, and how? What are our values?

What do we stand for?

Do you have a personal vision, mission, and values statement? If not, I suggest you write one. It can be short and simple – in fact, it should be short and simple.

Stick it on a wall where you will see it every day, or make it part of your computer's screensaver.

If it does its job, it will keep you focused, it will keep you doing the right things with your time, and it will keep you inspired.

Benjamin Franklin

*Either write something worth reading or
do something worth writing.*
— Benjamin Franklin

I love people with natural curiosity – people who look at the world around them and ask, "Why?" and then take the initiative to find out.

Benjamin Franklin's curiosity apparently knew few bounds, and through his entire 84 years, he put it to good work.

A successful entrepreneur, brilliant writer, satirist, politician, scientist, inventor, printer, thinker, defender, musician – there were few things that Mr. Franklin did not do.

Along the way he helped create the foundations of America, change the face of world power, and set a moral and ethical standard of conduct that, were more of today's leaders to follow it, the world would be a better place.

Ben took to heart the idea of the mark of a leader. When he was just 22, he wrote his epitaph. Later in his life he changed it, but clearly he was envisioning a full and accomplished end, and working backwards from his vision.

Most everyone I know struggles to get what they want done in a day. I am one of them. There just isn't enough time.

But of course, that is relative. Some people manage to put enough into one life to fill ten normal lives. They have the same 24 hours in a day, same seven days in a week, as everyone else.

One of these people was Benjamin Franklin.

Born in Boston in 1706, Ben was the tenth of 17 children of a soapmaker. Needless to say, he was not born to wealth. Financial circumstances meant there was no chance for him to get an education, and since he loved to read (a recurring theme with our leaders), his father put him to work as an apprentice in the print shop of Ben's elder brother, James.

While carrying out his grueling work, young Ben soon learned that he loved to write as much as he loved to read. When he was just 15, he and James started Boston's first "newspaper," carrying news from abroad, opinion pieces, and ads.

Among the opinion pieces was a series of letters slipped under the door of the newspaper office by a woman named Silence Dogood. The letters expressed critical views of the world and particularly of the way women were treated. They were such a huge success that they drove newspaper sales.

When James discovered that Silence was none other than his 16-year-old sibling using a pseudonym, his jealousy sparked a feud that ultimately resulted in Ben's running away at the age of 17.

Franklin hopped a boat to New Jersey, where he was unable to find work, and continued on to Philadelphia. There he arrived in the middle of the night in a terrible storm, knowing no one and with no prospects for work. He had only a few pennies in his pockets, most of which he gave to a young woman he saw begging with her baby by the side of the road.

And so began one of the most remarkable careers of the last few centuries.

Since printing was his trade, he soon found work in that field and then got funding to open a print shop of his own. His tremendous work ethic attracted attention, and the diligent young man was rewarded with large contracts, particularly from the government. He soon married, opened a store beside his shop, and watched both undertakings flourish.

He believed passionately in the power of the press and the importance of bringing news to the people so they could be informed. In fact, he began including political cartoons in his paper (which he created himself) so that people who had not learned to read could sill get the important news.

The cartoons were evidence of a wicked sense of humor that he would use throughout his life. He became particularly adept at employing satire to lampoon the pretentiousness, social inequity, and self-indulgence that he saw in the world around him.

His success earned him the financial means to buy the *Philadelphia Gazette* at the ripe age of 23 (how many 23-year-old owners of major newspapers do you find today?), which quickly became the most successful newspaper in the colonies and gave him another important outlet for his insightful and intelligent opinions.

Just a few years later, he began publishing what is perhaps his best-known work, the annual *Poor Richard's Almanac*. In addition to weather predictions, the previous year's major news, and recipes, it contained much of Franklin's most famous and wittiest writing. In a colony of less than 15,000 people, Franklin sold 10,000 copies a year and became wealthy.

His work ethic was not focused simply on writing and publishing, however. His love of books spurred him to create the first public lending library.

That was simply the tip of the iceberg of his inventiveness. Franklin's natural curiosity drove him to find solutions to problems that he saw around him, with notable results.

His printing skills enabled him to print paper money and establish the paper currency system.

Tiring of constantly putting his own glasses on and off, he invented bifocals, with different lenses in the top and bottom for reading and distance.

Motivated by the desire to relieve a brother suffering from kidney stones, he invented the flexible urinary catheter.

He conducted the famous kite experiment, immortalized in several paintings, showing how electricity was attracted by and conducted through metal. This prompted him to invent the lightning rod, which continues to protect buildings and vehicles to this day.

He invented the Franklin stove, a way for people to heat their homes more safely than they could with open fireplaces. He also formed the first fire department in Philadelphia.

Fire was a constant threat, and when people lost their homes or farms to fire, they often could not afford to rebuild. So Franklin came up with the idea of a fund of money, to which everyone contributed, that would be used for rebuilding by victims of fires – a fund now known as fire insurance.

As Postmaster of Philadelphia he needed a pricing system based on the distance that mail had to be carried, so he invented the odometer.

He was a very accomplished musician, playing the violin, harp, and guitar. He also invented a remarkable instrument called the armonica, consisting of spinning glass wheels on whose rims the performer would "play" with a dampened finger. It gave a sound similar to what you can create on the rims of water glasses.

He was a great writer and published several books, including his classic autobiography – which I highly recommend – and a groundbreaking book on electricity.

But it was undoubtedly through his political career that he had the greatest influence on the world.

While he was active in Philadelphia his entire life, it was when he was in his later 40s that politics began to dominate his time. England still controlled the colonies, but it was becoming increasingly clear that England's practice of ruling from across the ocean and collecting stiff taxes in return for contributing nothing was a system that could not survive.

In 1757, in the run-up to the American Revolution, Franklin moved to London to represent the Pennsylvania Assembly in what became a battle for control of the colonies. He was there for close to 20 years, soon representing many jurisdictions in addition to Pennsylvania.

Seeing the corruption and myopic views of the wealthy land-owners and British royalty, he quickly became convinced that the colonies must unite and become independent. He returned to America and over the next few years helped do the political spadework to create an independent nation. He was the only man to be involved with and sign all four of the documents that helped form the United States: the Declaration of Independence, the Treaty of Alliance with France, the Treaty of Peace with Britain and France, and the Constitution.

Franklin's political career was the culmination of a life based on the deep philosophical belief that all people are created equal and deserve equal access to liberty and opportunity.

That simple philosophy was the underpinning of American independence.

Obviously his strong entrepreneurial spirit also fostered a belief in free enterprise – a belief that the way to a successful career and life was through hard work and discipline.

But all through his life he was devoted to doing right. One of his last public acts, in 1789, was to write a seminal anti-slavery treatise.

Benjamin Franklin came into the world the son of a simple soapmaker. When he died, in 1790, at the age of 84, an estimated 20,000 people attended his funeral. That represented over two-thirds of all the men, women, and children in Philadelphia at the time.

He left a mark materially, philosophically, politically, and spiritually all over the world. His work and thinking changed the face of the planet.

Mark Twain wrote a wonderful satirical essay in 1870 called "The Late Benjamin Franklin." In it, he complained that Franklin had ruined childhood for future generations by setting an example no one else could ever hope to live up to.

But in truth, Franklin has served as an inspiration for generations that have followed. *"Your net worth to the world,"* he said, *"is usually determined by what remains after your bad habits are subtracted from your good ones."*

Were he alive today he would tell us that one of the secrets of his putting so much into a single life was the good habit of planning his time meticulously. He carried a book with him everywhere in which he plotted his hours and recorded his thoughts. His method for having the time to do so much was simply not to waste any. And he was careful to allocate time to thinking, not just doing: a habit that many of us would do well to put to practice.

But the mark he has left on me was his curiosity and inventiveness, best summed up in this simple quotation: *"If you live every moment with joy and curiosity, time is merely an occasional inconvenience."*

Ponderables

Here are some of Franklin's best-known sayings:

A house is not a home unless it contains food and fire for the mind as well as the body.

A penny saved is a penny earned.

A man wrapped up in himself makes a very small bundle.

An investment in knowledge pays the best interest.

Be at war with your vices, at peace with your neighbors, and let every new year find you a better man.

Beer is living proof that God loves us and wants us to

be happy.

By failing to prepare, you are preparing to fail.

Having been poor is no shame, but being ashamed of it is.

I wake up every morning at nine and grab for the morning paper. Then I look at the obituary page. If my name is not on it, I get up.

If you know how to spend less than you get, you have the philosopher's stone.

In this world nothing can be said to be certain, except death and taxes.

It is easier to prevent bad habits than to break them.

It is the eye of other people that ruins us. If I were blind I would want neither fine clothes, fine houses, nor fine furniture.

Many a man thinks he is buying pleasure, when he is really selling himself to it.

Money never made a man happy yet, nor will it. The more a man has, the more he wants. Instead of filling a vacuum, it makes one.

Benjamin Franklin was one of the world's great time managers. One of his distinguishing characteristics was that he scheduled time for things other than "doing things" and "work." He scheduled time to think, to explore, and to learn.

Many of us with businesses get so caught up in running the business – in working "in" it – that we never get time for working "on" it. And if you are like most people, if you don't schedule the time, it simply will not happen.

How do you plan your time? Do you allocate time for thinking? For learning? For wandering around and talking to people? For goofing off and just exploring new things?

Do you allocate time to work out? To catch up or network with friends or associates? Or to shut down completely?

Benjamin Franklin admittedly lived in a much simpler era. But were he alive today, I have no doubt that he would still be tremendously effective. And I bet that one of the cornerstones of his success would be his relentless discipline in managing time.

You are what you make time for. Simple as that.

Sir Richard Branson
& Virgin

Business opportunities are like buses.
There's always another one coming.
– Sir Richard Branson

I love rebels – people who go against the status quo. It is from rebellious thought that all change is born. I will confess that I like my rebels within reason – those who choose guns and weapons of war are not on my list.

In business today I look for rebels whom I can follow, in part because there are so few. So much of business has been sanitized, so much of the adventure has been lost.

So as a rebel lover, it is hard for me not to be attracted to Sir Richard Branson. Handsome, long blonde hair, jeans not suits. Adventure lover, risk taker, drinker, and partier. A flirty, put-everything-you-have-into-every-moment, nothing's-too-much-if-it-gets-publicity, knighted-by-the-Queen-of-England, maverick kind of guy.

As it turns out, this rebel also has a finely tuned business instinct. He seems to have the Midas touch, for decades now turning a bunch of seemingly unrelated businesses into successes.

He would be the first to tell you he is just an ordinary guy who has some good instincts and doesn't like to stand still. He also loves playing the rebel.

He has played it to the hilt, lived a charmed life, and made a lot of money for a lot of people in the process.

While doing that, he has also made a lot of businesses better for us consumers because he has challenged the status quo.

As for changing the world – I think he's just beginning. I believe the third and fourth acts of Sir Richard will be even better than the first two.

There was a time when doing business was fun. My father used to price jobs for his customers on napkins while they enjoyed a martini together. The napkin and a handshake was all it took to seal the deal. The job was done on budget and to impeccable standards. Everyone was happy.

Today, as most companies get larger, they lose the fun – if they ever had it to begin with. Political correctness sets in, and the complexity of managing a lot of people creates bureaucracy. And on and on.

That is coupled, of course, with the prevalent belief, among a huge majority of adults, that as you get older you are supposed to stop having fun. It is sad but true. How many adults do you know who are fun (when they're sober)? Do we learn nothing from our kids about fun?

The Virgin Group is a notable exception to all this. A multi-billion-dollar empire that spans the globe and likes to have fun while making money.

Led by flamboyant founder Sir Richard Branson, Virgin is the young upstart – the hip Don Quixote fighting against large entrenched players on behalf of better customer service, lower prices, and, yes, fun.

Branson is the archetypical entrepreneur. He is the leader of a multibillion-dollar business, yet he strikes you as the kind of guy who would make a deal with you on a napkin while having a pint, shake your hand, and that would be it. He'd be off to his next adventure, and the deal would get done according to the terms on the napkin. And he'd talk to you as an equal and genuinely care about the answers to his questions.

He is a classic entrepreneurial success story – the kind that makes you just want to go out and start a business.

A dyslexic kid at a time when dyslexia wasn't understood,

he was taunted at school in his native England because he couldn't read or write well. It probably only set his resolve to prove himself.

He tells a story that reveals a lot about his character. When he was 15, on a family summer vacation, his aunt challenged him to learn to swim. He committed to doing so before the vacation was over, and she committed to giving him ten shillings if he was successful.

He tried and tried, but continually sank like a stone. His family resigned themselves to his losing the bet. But on the way home, the sea long behind them, their car passed a river. He insisted that his father stop, climbed out, tore off his clothes, and jumped into the water.

He knew that this river was his last chance for success. He thrashed and thrashed, to no avail, until he finally relaxed and let the current carry him. The light bulb went on, and he started moving his arms and legs, using the current as his support rather than as a force to be overcome.

Soon he was indeed swimming, to the cheers of his family. And the treasured ten shillings was his.

Never say never to an entrepreneur. Perhaps the most consistent feature of Branson's career is that he has succeeded when most people around him said that he could not. Because once he makes up his mind to do something, he does not give up.

In high school he started a small magazine. People said he was too young to run a business. He had no office but soon was selling 50,000 copies a month. His understanding of what people wanted was uncanny, and his instincts guided him to do what established magazines would not.

Inspired by a co-worker who said, "We're all virgins at business," he stumbled onto the name for his little publishing empire.

At 18, he started a mail-order record business and again went where no one else would – into the emerging punk and glam scenes. His first big hit was Mike Oldfield's *Tubular Bells*, which had been rejected by every serious label. It took off. He signed the Sex Pistols and Culture Club – again, groups that no serious record label would touch – and Virgin Records was flying.

He was always the brash young adventurer with a flair for the dramatic whom the establishment took only moderately seriously. Until one day he signed the Rolling Stones, the most coveted act in rock-'n'-roll at the time. Amid gasps of astonishment, the establishment suddenly knew that Branson was a force to be reckoned with.

From records it was on to airlines, as well as trains, telecom, cosmetics, bridal gowns, balloon rides, health clubs, and many other businesses. Today the Virgin Group is made up of hundreds of companies, many of them very small but collectively amassing more than eight billion dollars a year in sales. All of them think and act as fiercely independently as Branson does.

He has had more than his share of failures, including the very high-profile Virgin Cola. But failure has never slowed him down. Trying is as important as winning in his world. He hates to sit still and hates even more the thought of missing any great experience in his life. Had Nike not come up with the slogan first, his would be, "Just do it."

He moves quickly – an impossibility for most large companies. His friend Nelson Mandela told him of a chain of health clubs in South Africa that was going out of business, putting thousands of people out of work. He wondered if Richard would be interested in the investment. Branson boarded a plane, looked at the books, liked what he saw, and bought the chain immediately. Today he owns the majority of health clubs in South Africa.

While becoming one of the world's most successful businessmen – and being knighted (there's a paradox) – he has become one of the world's greatest adventurers. He has attempted to circumnavigate the globe in a balloon, barely surviving. He has crossed the Atlantic in a speedboat and in a balloon. And he was the founding sponsor of the first private rocket to break out of earth's atmosphere, Spaceship One.

Is space flight on Virgin's agenda? You bet, in the form of an undertaking called Virgin Galactic. It is a matter of "when" not "if."

His adventurous spirit has made its mark on Virgin and is a hallmark of his success. His PR stunts to launch new companies are the stuff of legend. He jumps, he flies, he climbs, he dances – the bigger, the crazier, the more politically incorrect, and the more fun, the more likely he is to do it.

There is not another CEO on this planet who would do what Richard Branson does as part of running his business. And that is one of the secrets of Virgin's success. They do what no one else will do.

Branding experts say you cannot carry a brand name across as many businesses as Virgin does. The brand, say the experts, gets diluted until it stands for nothing. Yet Virgin continually proves this theory wrong.

And surely that's another secret of their success. With no business school training, Sir Richard hasn't been brainwashed into believing that certain things can or can't be done. So he is free to go and find out for himself, trusting his gut rather than what a professor says.

They said he couldn't compete with British Airways, but he did. They said he couldn't compete with the big telecom players, but he did. Cosmetics, health clubs, trains, banking. At every step people said, "You can't do that," and he proved them wrong.

His fundamental belief in business is to look for opportunities where the established players are doing a bad job, or where a market is not being served. Do your homework and then move quickly.

In 1996, while Virgin was experiencing tremendous growth, Branson took it public. Of course the offer sold out almost instantly. But the processes of a public company, with every major decision requiring board approval, stifled the very heart and soul of the company. He was also anguished by the fact that, as the company's share price dropped at the whim of the brokerage community, small investors were suffering.

So he bought the shares back and took the company private again. He says the move was a tremendous relief, because he was once again the master of his own fate.

You can tell a lot about a company by observing its leader. This is equally true of small startups and big public multinationals. Virgin is a bold, brash, risk-taking entity that likes nothing better than to take on giants and outthink them, out hustle them, and outwork them for customers and market share.

Branson takes chances and relies on his gut, like most entrepreneurs. But he carefully gathers facts and evaluates the odds before making decisions. He may gamble, but he understands the odds before he puts his money down.

Yet for all its bravado, Virgin knows that it is not solving the world's problems and so does not take itself too seriously.

Rather like its leader.

Branson is no public speaker. He is self-effacing and rather quiet in front of a crowd. He is far more comfortable with a drink and a few people in front of him than on a stage. He takes cabs, has no driver, and avoids many of the typical trappings of wealth like private planes and large yachts (though he does, famously, own a private island in the Caribbean).

He also has a tireless work ethic. He is always on the go, citing his ability to take catnaps for an hour or two as one of the key reasons he gets as much done as he does.

His entrepreneurial style and that of the Virgin companies holds lessons for anyone aspiring to start a business or currently involved with one. Here is Branson's view of the vision and position of Virgin in the market:

> *I think one of the reasons for our success is the core values which Virgin aspires to, like providing quality service. However, we also promise value for money, and we try to do things in an innovative way in areas where consumers are often ripped off or not getting the most for their money. I believe we should do what we do with a sense of fun and without taking ourselves too seriously, too! If Virgin stands for anything, it should be for not being afraid to try out new ideas in new areas.*

Every company in business wants to innovate. But few really have the stomach for it. There are very few breakthrough products in any market because taking big risks is just not in the DNA of most companies. Which really means not in the DNA of most leaders.

I think the mark of Sir Richard Branson lies in a simple understanding of character.

With all due respect to the Harvard School of Business, you can't teach passion or fun. The history of the world has been written by people who were unafraid to take risks and who touched other people in their hearts, not just their heads. Logic may give you the reason to try something new, but it's your heart that will make you get off the couch and do it, and then will keep you doing it when success seems impossible.

Sadly, at most large corporations today, there just isn't much passion. Lots of left-brained approaches to management and leadership, but not a lot that really talks to the imagination or the heart.

Some of Branson's detractors mock his antics. But I argue that they are missing one of the most important ingredients of a great leader. If you can get people's hearts to go somewhere, their heads will follow. The opposite just isn't true.

And, surely, creating an organization whose ethos is contagious – to its employees and to its customers – is the goal of every business person.

Ponderables

The great businesswoman Mary Kay Ash once said, *"The speed of the leader is the speed of the gang."* How right she was.

You can see the style, personality, and speed of any team or organization in its leader. Here are a few questions or challenges I like to ask about leadership style.

Describe your leadership style in five words or less.

If you had to draw a picture of your organization, what would it look like?

If you were to pick a pop song as your company's theme, what song would it be, and why?

Other than to get paid, why should people follow you?

Describe your perfect workplace environment. Are you creating it?

If you could do any job in the world other than the one you are doing, what would it be?

Howard Schultz
& Starbucks

I believe life is a series of near misses. A lot of what we ascribe to luck is not luck at all. It's seizing the day and accepting responsibility for your future. It's seeing what other people don't see and pursuing that vision.

– Howard Schulz

I have often joked with friends that the solution to world peace would be to get rid of coffee. Caffeine is a powerful drug to which many of us get addicted in our youth, or while cramming for college exams. It makes some people crazy, and I am one of them.

So all over the Middle East, where tensions run highest, what are people drinking? Coffee and cola? How smart is that? Let's all get buzzed and scream at each other – that will solve the problem.

On a serious note, coffee is here to stay. So is tea. So if you are going to have either, you may as well have a good one in a nice place.

This is the story of a brand that agrees with me.

What I love about this story is that almost anyone can make a cup of coffee or tea. Grind beans or get a tea bag, add hot water, and presto – hot beverage.

How tough is that?

So, how do you turn beans or tea leaves and water into one of the world's greatest and most valuable brands?

Here's how. It is a wonderful story of a team with a passion and a mission, a tremendous set of values from which they refuse to stray to this day, and a public that was waiting for a better mousetrap.

A mile in under four minutes? Impossible. People flying like birds? Impossible. Sending pictures and sound on invisible waves through the air? Impossible. Buying things over the Internet? Impossible. Five bucks for a cup of coffee? **Impossible!**

"The greater the opportunity," said James Cook, *"the fewer are those who see it."*

Coffee was once a simple commodity in North America. A watery concoction undifferentiated by taste, quality, or price.

To a marketer, that's a great opportunity. And the opportunist came in the form of a young man from the Bronx projects, Howard Schultz.

Schultz was a seemingly typical kid from a blue collar family. He had worked his way through college, been a half-decent football player, and was now a seemingly normal middle-class guy raising a young family and selling kitchen appliances in New York.

One day in 1981 he noticed that a tiny customer in Seattle was buying more drip coffee makers than even large stores like Macy's. He was curious – who were they, and what were they doing to sell so many coffee makers?

Like all great leaders, rather than just wonder, he took action and jumped on a plane to get an answer.

The customer was a small outfit named Starbucks, which sold bags of coffee in a tiny store in Pike Place Market. What struck Schultz was that, when it came to coffee, the owners were not just passionate, they were evangelistic. They were like coffee sommeliers.

Their Arabica-only beans came from exotic locations around the world, and were roasted dark, unlike light American coffee. It gave their product a full, rich flavor, far different from any-thing Schultz had ever tasted before.

In one moment he fell in love with their product. He approached the owners and tried to convince them to make him their first director of marketing. His passion told him that he could help make them into something much bigger.

They politely turned him down.

It took him a year of trying until they finally relented. He packed up his young family and moved to Seattle.

Schultz had the right idea: a product whose quality was head and shoulders above its competition. He saw the possibility of changing how Americans thought of coffee. But he knew that to do that – to create a brand that resonated with people – he had to find a way for them to connect with coffee emotionally.

Some people believe in chance. Others believe that important incidents happen in our lives every day – we're just usually too busy to notice.

Schultz's "chance" came on a business trip to Milan a year or so later. While walking the streets, he was struck by how many cafés there were, seemingly one on every corner. Inside, staff called baristas were making their huge coffee machines whirr and clunk as they turned out espressos and cappuccinos for lineups of eager Italians.

What was even more striking to Schultz was that these café bars, with standup counters and few tables and seats, were neighborhood gathering places. There, locals would meet on the way to work, at lunch, and in the evening. They would have a coffee and maybe a light snack, and talk. It was a routine. A deep and meaningful part of their daily lives.

And in a moment, Schultz knew that he had found his answer. To change how Americans thought of coffee, he needed to connect with them at the soulular level.

He would do that by introducing his customers to the

centuries-old romance of coffee and the social aspects of drinking coffee with friends. Starbucks would be a neighborhood gathering place where people would go to have a cup of great coffee or tea, meet their friends and talk, escape from it all and relax, or even do some quiet work.

Starbucks' owners turned his idea down.

Fortunately for many of us, Schultz had the courage not to quit, and the passion for his new business idea to get others to listen, believe him, and support him.

Using some borrowed money and his mortgage, he opened up his own little Italian-style café, Il Giornale.

He worked his butt off, dealing with all the worry and self-doubt of a typical entrepreneur – uncertain of the future and with the pressure of a young family to support. He sought financing and was rejected hundreds of times.

But he was bold. He had a vision of opening stores in every major American city. He got a friend to do a projection spreadsheet based on opening 75 stores in five years – and scaled it back to 50 because he didn't think anyone would believe him.

His hard work paid off and he opened a second café. And then opportunity knocked.

Word was out that the owners of Starbucks wanted to get out of their six Seattle stores and their roasting plant. They could be added to Il Giornale's three stores.

Schultz sprang into action and pulled together some private financing. In an ironic twist, he bought Starbucks from the very people who had rejected his idea of a premium coffee chain.

And thus began the rocket ride of one of the world's most powerful and valuable brands.

Starbucks is an impeccably run company. That has allowed them to grow at blazing speed while creating a consistently high-quality product and experience at every location.

They are completely clear on their vision. They are fanatical about product quality, and sometimes uncompromising to a fault.

But the Starbucks secret goes much deeper than great product.

They have differentiated a commodity – coffee – by making the simple act of purchasing and drinking it an experience. A premium experience.

Everything about their organization, from the stores to their merchandising, graphics, communication, and packaging, is done masterfully to impeccable standards. They are brilliant and disciplined marketers and among the best brand builders in business history.

They make you want to go to their coffee shops, the first time usually by word of mouth and PR, but thereafter because of the product and the experience.

Amazingly, Starbucks spent only $10 million on advertising

in all the years up to 1998. That's the power of word of mouth when you have a great product.

Once you're there, they make you want to stay. They have recreated the romance Schultz saw in Milan and made it not only better in most cases, but uniquely theirs. The look, the feel, the aroma – all stimulate your senses.

But at the root of it all is people – their people, their customers, and their suppliers and communities around the world. As senior team member Howard Behar said of Starbucks, *"We're not in the coffee business. We're in the people business serving coffee."*

Early on, Starbucks realized that it would be their people who would make the experience successful. The people in head office. The people inside every store. The people around the world who grow the coffees that they buy. And the people in every community they touch.

Their commitment to all of these people is deeply ingrained in the organization's culture. In the late 1980s, they were the first company of their kind to extend health-care benefits to part-time employees – a huge financial commitment, since part-timers were two-thirds of their workforce. It was done because they genuinely do care – starting with Schultz, who has never forgotten his roots.

The payback for this commitment has been immense. And today, a visit to virtually any Starbucks will show you that their commitment is still strong.

The staff is friendly and well-trained. The baristas are performers, the machines and cups their tools, the customers their audience. They understand the power of stories. And they understand that the interaction between customers and baristas is the single most important part of the Starbucks experience.

Inside their stores, you can also see the story of Starbucks in the communities from which they buy their products. They are committed to paying a fair price for product, supporting the communities that support them, and being environmentally responsible in everything they do. Some companies do this because they believe it is good for their business. Starbucks does it because they believe it.

And finally, their commitment to people ultimately comes down to customers and how they serve them.

Starbucks, for many, is what sociologists call a Third Place, behind only the home and office in importance to their customers. *"We're not filling bellies. We're filling souls,"* says Behar.

Consequently, their customers are fiercely loyal. The bond between brand and customer is so powerful that Starbucks has even created its own vocabulary: "Vente dry soy caramel frappuccino, please." Very few brands in the cluttered market of today have the power to do that as Starbucks has.

Imagine how it annoys their competition every time a Starbucks customer comes in and asks for a "vente."

And of course, they have proven that if you give your customers a product and an experience they love, price is not an issue. Most of their customers simply don't care.

Starbucks' unique relationship with their customers has allowed them to diversify their product offering, expanding into areas no one would have guessed just a few years ago.

Seeing their customers' passion for music, they started selling Starbucks-compiled CDs at the counter. Today, Starbucks' Hear Music is a thriving part of the business that not only has a range of its own unique branded titles, but often outsells traditional music retailers with new releases.

Noticing that customers used their stores as offices, Starbucks pioneered installing wireless Internet access in its stores. Today it is hard to find a Starbucks without a mobile worker sipping a drink while working at a laptop.

At some Starbucks locations, technology and music come together with rows of listening stations where customers can burn their own custom music CDs.

And you can pay for it all, of course, with a Starbucks debit or credit card.

With the depth of customer loyalty that they have built, the possibilities for the brand are huge.

Today Starbucks is opening new stores at a phenomenal rate. To date, the speed has had no negative impact on their ability to deliver a first-class experience consistently around the world.

For those locations where a store doesn't make sense, the sign "We Proudly Brew Starbucks" is a huge welcome for Starbucks junkies.

And what is the mark of Starbucks? Is it just another success-ful global corporation squeezing out the little coffee houses? I don't think so. It is quite the opposite.

Starbucks has not won by slashing prices, squeezing grow-ers, and driving or buying local coffee shops out of business. Starbucks has won because they have a powerful vision and because they are relentless about quality in everything they do.

And what exactly is wrong with rewarding that? It is what every business is supposed to do.

Ponderables

A "brand" is defined as the sum total of experiences and perceptions people have of a product or service. The perceptions of a brand are shaped by the experiences one has with it, directly or indirectly.

Companies spend millions and, in some cases, even billions of dollars refining their brands in the market in order to influence people to buy them.

Starbucks has clearly differentiated itself in the mar-ket by the experience they create: their product qual-ity, their approach to people, and their commitment to their communities and the environment.

Any of us as individuals can think the same way Star-bucks does. We are "people brands."

How do you differentiate yourself – what is unique about the brand that is you?

If you were to write a brand statement for yourself, what would it say?

What things about yourself would you never compromise?

Describe the experience of those dealing with you: at work, at home, in your community.

What will your obituary say about the brand called "you"?

Steve Jobs
& Apple Computer

*Do you want to sell sugared water for the rest of
your life or change the world?*
– Steve Jobs

Why is it that every product that comes out of
Apple Computer is so elegant – in look, feel, and
function?

Why has Apple always been the pioneer to show us
new futures – in publishing, graphics, multimedia,
music, and video?

Why are they the only company in the tech sector
that is consistently "cool," and has been since at least
1984?

Why is Pixar the greatest animation studio of our
time, producing an unbroken string of blockbuster
movies that parents love as much as their kids do?
Why was Pixar so far ahead of the industry that their
geniuses are now calling the shots at Disney's animation studios?

Why is it that while the music labels and entertainment companies were trying to close down Napster
and sue an entire generation of kids for copyright

violation, it was Apple that came up with a viable vision for the future of music distribution?

Why was it a computer company, Apple, that figured out how to make music personal and portable with its iPod in a way that no one had done before?

The answer is leadership.

These companies have in common not only teams of incredibly talented, hardworking, and visionary people who are passionate about changing the world for the better. They also have in common Steve Jobs, unquestionably one of the greatest and highest-impact business visionaries of the last several decades.

Steve Jobs set out to change the world. And he has done just that!

With the question, *"Do you want to sell sugared water for the rest of your life or change the world?"* Steve Jobs, then CEO of Apple Computer, made perhaps the greatest pitch of all time in a job interview.

The interview was with John Sculley, then a senior Pepsi

executive, whom Jobs had been trying to lure to Apple to become CEO. Steve had been unsuccessful in wooing Sculley until he finally put the situation in those crystal-clear terms.

Once the choice was set forth with that clarity, Sculley's pride and sense of destiny could not refuse, and he took the job.

Steve Jobs is not an angel as a manager, according to many who have worked with him. He has made his share of mistakes, both personal and professional. So have I. But I would put to you that there are few business leaders like him in history who can match him for coming up with powerful and compelling visions and turning them into products.

Absolute clarity about the vision is essential to great leadership. But a clear and compelling vision is very difficult to originate and maintain in a large corporation. There are just too many people to please.

The passion and vision of most garage startups is usually lost once those startups get large. The price of success is political correctness, org charts, and quarterly targets. It is particularly painful when those large companies go public.

There are very few "cool" multibillion-dollar companies that can manage the magic troika of passionate customers, passionate channel partners, and passionate employees.

Then there are the companies of Steve Jobs.

His mantra has been to make not great products but "insanely great" products – products that change the world. And his track record in doing so is formidable.

Apple's brand has always been characterized by breakthrough. By being the best in their market. By taking risks and igniting passion.

They have done it with hardware: the original Apple, the Apple II, the Mac, the iPod.

They have done it with software: the desktop publishing market, desktop music creation and production, the music download market, and the desktop video production and editing market.

They have had their failures, to be sure. But today, almost 40 years after they started, they are one of the world's top ten brands by any important measure.

Why? How have they survived when so many others have failed?

Because Apple and Steve Jobs have never lost their vision of insanely great products. The company is driven by product innovation. It is micromanaged by its leader, probably to a fault. They are relentless in their efforts to improve design to make products more intuitive, easier to use, better looking, better feeling in the hand.

They are not afraid to take chances – to lead the market rather than be led by it. And they know that their loyal customers will forgive them a few mistakes.

It's in their DNA.

You can criticize Steve Jobs all you want, but you cannot argue with his success as a leader where it counts in business – results. Through the ups and downs, the ins and outs, like the proverbial cat, he has always landed back on his feet.

I would argue that he, and his teams, have always had a clear understanding of their vision, their raison d'etre.

In the world of corporate branding, there is a phrase called "the elevator test." The idea is that if someone asks you what you or your company does when you meet them in an elevator, you must be able to articulate the answer within just a few floors of the ride. Your answer must be compelling enough that they want to know more and ask you to follow up.

This is the goal of most advertising – to make you want to buy a product or service, or at least want to know more about it, all in 30 or 60 seconds.

You can't have a great elevator speech without a clear vision. Ninety percent of the world's companies don't. Apple does, and always has.

Here is perhaps their most famous story of the power of a great elevator speech drawn from a clear vision.

The year was 1983. The computer market was a very different place back then, and the computer was a very different thing.

With its Apple and Apple II products, Apple had been one of

the first serious players in the personal computer market. In addition to "insanely great" products, they had a vision that everyone would one day have their own personal computer. It was a vision shared, though seen somewhat differently, by Bill Gates and his Microsoft Corporation.

This was a revolutionary idea at a time when computers filled huge climate-controlled rooms.

The real competition for Apple at the time was the IBM PC, sold by a sales force who, back then, wore blue suits and white shirts as a mandatory dress code.

IBM owned the corporate market because of its mainframe business, and had very low expectations of how many of its personal computers it would actually sell. Still, it was a giant, and its marketing strength was undeniable.

The industry standard operating system was Microsoft's DOS – green letters on a black screen, no graphics, no mouse, and a lot of arcane commands. To get anything done, the user had to memorize the commands or have a cheat sheet beside the computer.

On a visit to the Xerox Palo Alto Research Center lab, Steve Jobs had seen prototypes of a device called a mouse, and computers that had graphic interfaces – graphic pictures – instead of lines of green type. He knew this was the future of computing.

He went to work creating a version of what he had seen. In fact, two teams were formed at Apple: one working on a computer called Lisa, the other, headed by Jobs, working on the Macintosh.

Talk about clarity of vision. The Mac team, a bunch of young geniuses who would work all day and night to fulfill the destiny of the Mac, was symbolized by a pirate flag hanging on their building.

When your flag is the Jolly Roger, there is not a lot of doubt about your culture.

The Mac was ready to launch in late 1983. It was decided to introduce it in January during the Super Bowl, the event that would bring the most attention to the new product in the fastest way possible.

A 60-second slot was purchased by Apple's brilliant ad agency, Chiat Day. Apple then charged them with coming up with creative ads worthy of this world-changing product.

Twenty years later, the folklore surrounding the commercial is hard to differentiate from the fact. Suffice it to say that the creative team put forth several ideas, including one for a take-off on George Orwell's famous book *1984*.

In the concept, Big Brother would be IBM and the Macintosh would be the rebel who would break the world free of its tyrannical chains. It would be "the computer for the rest of us."

It was a bold, risky concept. Apple would be David, throwing a stone right in the eye of Goliath. Whom would it offend? How would IBM respond?

The idea was rejected by Apple.

Chiat Day came back again and again with new ideas, and a young creative champion kept resubmitting the bold *1984* idea until Apple finally relented and approved it.

Ridley Scott of *Blade Runner* fame was hired as film director. The commercial was made at great expense and to the highest cinematic standards. The agency was proud of its work of art and showed it to the client for approval.

Apple's board of directors saw it and immediately panicked. Fear set in. It was too risky, too bold, and too in-your-face. They intervened and asked the ad agency to sell the Super Bowl airtime.

Chiat Day tried to sell the 60 seconds of media, the most expensive airtime in the world, but could not find any buyers. So on the Friday preceding the Sunday event, Apple had a choice: run the commercial or run nothing. The cost was the same either way.

Apple decided to run the commercial. It was the single most significant decision they ever made.

The commercial showed a room of dreary, dronelike people sitting in a huge hall listening to the ranting of their Big Brother leader on a giant monochromatic screen. *"We are one people. With one will. One resolve. One cause. Our enemies shall talk themselves to death. And we will bury them with their own confusion,"* preached their leader from the screen. *"We shall prevail."*

Into the hall burst an athletic young woman carrying a sledge-hammer and chased by police. She ran to the front of the crowd of drones and, with great drama, flung the sledgehammer into the video screen, exploding the image of Big Brother and sending smoke and wind whirling through the room.

Superimposed on the open-mouthed drones came this copy, read by an announcer: *"On January 24, Apple Computer will introduce Macintosh. And you'll see why 1984 won't be like 1984."*

In 60 seconds, in what is regarded by many as the greatest TV commercial ever created, Apple positioned itself and divided the entire market into "them" – the drones who follow IBM – and "us" – the vibrant, alive, free thinkers who would use a Macintosh.

In 60 seconds, because of the clarity of their vision and the story they used to tell it, they forced the audience – millions of people – to choose sides. Them or us?

The commercial ran once and was never aired again until a slightly altered version was used for the iPod almost 20 years later.

In 60 seconds Apple created a market for the Mac. And with it, because of the power of their vision, they created the foundation of a customer base that remains perhaps the most loyal and passionate in the world.

The Macintosh changed the world. With its graphics, its mouse, its built-in sound, and on and on. It was the first user-friendly computer, and its impact was staggering.

The Mac forced the entire computer industry to change.

When John Sculley and the board drove Steve Jobs out of Apple in 1985, they did not understand the power of visionary leadership. Apple fell on a decade of disasters and paid for it dearly in failed products, lost market share, and a revolving door for their best employees.

It was Steve Jobs' powerful vision and fanatical attention to quality and detail that had driven Apple's successes. The leader and the brand were, and are, inexorably intertwined.

When Jobs returned to Apple in 1997 – after creating the foundation for another monster success at his little computer graphics company, Pixar – the passion and the vision were reignited.

If you have ever had doubts about the power of a leader to change a corporation, you need look no further than this.

Apple Computer has its flaws, like every corporation. But even a cynic would have a difficult time denying that their products are consistently among the best-designed in the world, that they have an incredibly loyal customer base, and that their market capitalization puts a huge multiple on their share price.

And I would argue that in the more than 20 years since the 1984 commercial aired, Steve Jobs has never strayed far from being the leader who rallied his Mac team to work all night by hoisting a Jolly Roger to remind them of what they stood for.

Very few individuals are as closely associated with their public companies as Jobs is. And Wall Street reasonably wonders what will happen to Apple once he is no longer at the helm.

But in the meantime, Apple continues to be a pioneer, to go where others have not gone before, and to make products that others copy and few surpass.

And what is the mark of Steve Jobs?

I think it is the simple strength of a powerful and compelling vision.

"Insanely great." "The computer for the rest of us." "Sugared water or change the world?"

If you can articulate exactly what you stand for, and you stick to your guns, anything is possible. Even a young woman taking on Big Brother ... and changing the world.

Ponderables

What is your elevator speech for your company, product, or service?

Imagine that your biggest competitor is given un-limited resources and budget to wipe your company or product right out of the market. If you were the competition, what would you do? How would you defend yourself against them?

Here is a personal scenario that I love to use: You have an opportunity to get the perfect, ideal dream job. You are asked to submit a 60-second commercial for yourself. Describe the dream job. Then write and visualize the script for that commercial.

Conclusion

The fact that no one understands you
doesn't make you an artist.
– Unknown

What Is Your Story?

Everything's a story. My life. Your life. Your kid's life.
Your career.
You name it, it's a story.

Stories have been the glue binding civilizations together since humans began communicating.

Sadly, the power of story has slipped out of most corporations and many civilizations these days. It needs to be reignited. Perhaps this book can help.

I believe that we all choose the way we frame our lives. We tend to create metaphors that become the lenses through which we see life.

Life is fun. Life is a challenge. Life is a game. Life is a battle.

I choose this:

"My Life is a great story, which I am writing."

I find "story" to be a powerful and empowering metaphor. When you view your life as a story, and accept that you are the author, you cannot be a victim.

You force yourself to be accountable. You force yourself to take action, unless your story happens to be about a couch potato, in which case, I would argue, the accountability has not yet kicked in.

If you are writing a story – **your story** – then you're in control. You control the plot. You control the central character. You write what you do and say, and how you do and say it. You create **you.**

Just as the cells in your body are constantly regenerating and replacing old with new, you are constantly writing the evolving story of you.

And you also control the other characters in your story and the relationships you have with them.

Who is a major character, and who isn't? Who is in for the long haul, and who will soon be just a memory? Who is good for you, and who is a drain on your energy and outcomes? Who is of good intent, and who has other motives?

You can't control **everything** that happens in your story. There is a force called life – the Universe. It seems to have a mind of its own that we can, at best, influence.

All to say that, at the very least, you can control how you respond to what life throws at you, good or bad.

In fact, one could easily argue that our stories as humans are universally about what we do with the talents we are given, the path we choose, and how we **respond** to what life throws at us along the path.

So what is the story **you** are writing?
What is the story your kids are writing?
What difference will you make?
What mark will you leave?
What mark will they leave?

What Is Your Mark?

After toiling over a work, the artist's last act is to put their signature on the work.

In doing so, the artist says, "I created this. It represents my skill, my imagination, my creativity." They make their mark and then put their work out there for the public and critics to judge, positively or otherwise.

Some business people scoff at the life of an artist, thinking it would be wonderful to paint all day. But I wonder how many of them would just as willingly sign **their** canvas, which is every day at work.

How many of you would say, "This day and all the things I did today represent my skill, my imagination, my creativity. If this day is all there is, I will gladly leave it as my mark."

Perhaps this simple thought is the foundation of leadership: committing not just to finishing a day, but to finishing a day that you will sign and leave as your mark.

Picasso understood this deeply.

As well as creating some of the greatest paintings and sculptures in history, Picasso also made simple sketches in a flash, without lifting his hand off the paper.

These "simple" sketches commanded incredible sums of money. People would gasp when they saw the price, and ask him, "How long did it take you to do that?" – as if the price and the time he took to do it were directly related.

Picasso knew exactly how long it took him before he signed his name.

"My whole life," was his answer.

And I believe that this simple concept is deeply understood by everyone I have profiled in this book.

I hope you have been inspired.

I hope you have learned something you did not know before.

I hope you will be prompted to make a mark in a way that is your own.

And I hope you will sign today, tomorrow, and the rest of the days of your life.

Thanks

Writing a book is a minor act of insanity. I have always had a profound respect for writers. It is now even greater.

The Mark of a Leader project – the book, the videos, the shows and seminars – has been a labor of love by a lot of people. And I owe them all deeply.

My parents, Gerry and Joyce, were role models I still emulate.

My beloved wife, Pam, has been a huge supporter, without whom this would still be just another idea. Thanks, baby.

My son, Matti, has been my inspiration and fresh eyes, and has taught me the meaning of unconditional love. Not bad for a five year old.

To the rest of my family, thanks for your never-ending enthusiasm and love.

Amanda, as usual, nothing would have happened without you. Thanks for so many great years and for keeping me honest.

Roma, thanks for your endless patience and great attitude.

Thanks to the great book team who brought this to life: Arnold Gosewich, who hung in with me for so long; Don Bastian, an incredible editor; Jaimie Heinke, wonderful researcher; and Steve Beinicke, designer extraordinaire.

Thanks to Gil Tam for the inspired logo and Dave Luxton for the great web design.

Thanks to Simon Edwards and Mike Stanutz for the amazing sounds.

To Tony Chapman and all my friends at Chopper, Lift, LiQuid, and Spinglobe, thank you for believing and helping us get here.

To my friends and colleagues Mark Victor Hansen, Robert Allen, Pat and Michelle Burns, and the Inner Circle – you are profound and wonderful friends and mentors who are changing the world for the better.

Thanks to all the clients who have used **The Mark of a Leader** and have spread the word. You are without exception amazing people and teams.

Thanks to Dana Atchley, the original Digital Storyteller. I am doing my best to keep your dream alive.

And, finally, thanks to everyone at ICE. Most of what I know about leadership I learned firsthand from you. That was one remarkable journey.

Please Send Us Your Leadership Stories

This book is Volume One of a series.

Doubtless you have ideas of leaders who could be included in future volumes or in our live event and video programs. Maybe they are famous. Maybe they are not. Maybe they are family members or friends, or on your team or in your business.

What they are is leaders – people, teams, and companies who have done or are doing something extraordinary to change lives, communities, or even the world.

Please let us know. Maybe they should be part of **The Mark of a Leader** as it grows.

Please send us your stories at our website:
www.themarkofaleader.com

We hope you enjoy this exciting journey with us!

The Mark of a Leader

The Mark of a Leader